Exploring Cinema Memory

Annette Kuhn is Emeritus Professor in Film Studies at Queen Mary University of London, a Fellow of the British Academy and a Member of the European Academy. She was Director of Cinema Culture in 1930s Britain and has published widely in the areas of cultural theory, film history and cultural memory, including *Family Secrets: Acts of Memory and Imagination* (2002); *An Everyday Magic: Cinema and Cultural Memory* (2002); *Locating Memory: Photographic Acts* (2006, co-edited with Kirsten Emiko McAllister); *Little Madnesses: Winnicott, Transitional Phenomena and Cultural Experience* (2013); *Memory Studies* special issue on Cinemagoing, Film Experience and Memory (2017, co-edited with Daniel Biltereyst and Philippe Meers); *Ratcatcher* (2020); and *Oxford Dictionary of Film Studies* (2020, co-authored with Guy Westwell).

Exploring Cinema Memory

Annette Kuhn

ARGYLL PUBLISHING

© Annette Kuhn 2023

First published by
Argyll Publishing
an imprint of Thirsty Books
www.thirstybooks.com

The author has asserted her moral rights.

British Library Cataloguing-in-Publication Data.
A catalogue record for this book in available from the British Library.

ISBN 978 1 7399922 9 3

Typeset & design: derek.rodger21@outlook.com

Printing: Bell & Bain Ltd, Glasgow

*To the men and women
who generously shared their cinemagoing memories.*

A children's matinee: 'On Saturday mornings we'd all go to the cinema'

Contents

Foreword by Daniel Biltereyst	9
Acknowledgements	11
1. Exploring Cinema Memory: An Introduction	15
2. Place and Time in Cinema Memory	27
3. What to do with Cinema Memory	41
4. Home Is Where We Start From	63
5. From Cinema Culture to Cinema Memory	79
6. The Bridge and the Passport	97
Appendix 1 Cinema Culture in 1930s Britain: Academic Publications	111
Appendix 2 The Cinema Memory Archive	117
Bibliography	121
Index	131

Foreword

WHEN thinking about how to understand the imaginative power of cinema, I always come back to a thought-provoking metaphor used by the Belgian surrealist artist René Magritte. In one of his later interviews Magritte, a lifelong passionate cinemagoer, referred to cinema as a trampoline for his own imagination. For him, going to the movies was much more than just a joyful pastime. Like art, Magritte claimed, cinema had the power of liberating revelation – and cinema triggered his imagination. In his paintings, he intermingled intimate personal memories with recollections of images, characters and stories he had seen in the cinema. Going to the cinema and seeing films opened up new worlds for Magritte, stimulating his imagination and inspiring him to create uncanny, sublime dream-like worlds where personal and cultural memories coalesced.

Few writers have been as influential and productive as Annette Kuhn in exploring ordinary people's engagement with cinema. In particular, her pioneering study of cinemagoing and cinema culture in Britain in the 1930s continues to inspire those seeking to understand the social and cultural meanings of cinema. Her book *An Everyday Magic: Cinema and Cultural Memory* remains among the most frequently cited works on film and cinema history, especially within the growing field of research on audiences' past experiences of film and cinema. Kuhn's subtle writings on these topics explore the multifaceted relationships between films, the filmic imagination and people's engagements with films on the one hand and social practices and remembered experiences of cinemagoing on the other.

This wonderful new collection of writings illustrates Kuhn's continuing attempts to unravel cinema memory as a very unique subtype of cultural memory. The essays can be read as a bid to create and refine a vocabulary that enables us to talk more clearly and evocatively about people's experience of cinema. Over the years Kuhn has enriched our vocabulary with such concepts and typologies as 'cinema memory', 'remembered images/scenes', 'situated memories', 'memories of cinemagoing', 'place-memory', 'memory maps' and 'topographical remembering'.

Exploring Cinema Memory comprises some of Kuhn's most seminal writings, carefully revised and updated, augmented by previously unpublished writings. One of the strengths of this work is that these delicately written essays are firmly based in robust and methodologically ambitious empirical research. In her ethnohistorical explorations of the interrelationship between cinema and memory, Kuhn draws on a combination of interviews, questionnaires and other informant-generated material (such as people's letters and essays describing their favourite cinemas, stars, or films) alongside contemporary source materials including fan magazines, the popular press, official reports and historical surveys.

This new collection also contains thoughtful reflections on the conceptual and methodological trajectory that has led the author and her co-workers to embrace the tools of digital humanities. The recently launched Cinema Memory and the Digital Archive project (CMDA) and its internet presence now offer ready access to the original data and findings of Kuhn's groundbreaking study of cinema culture in 1930s Britain. What emerges from its delightful website and from this new collection of essays is an unbound adventurous exploration of, and a continuously renewed quest to understand, the place of visual and popular culture in people's lives.

Daniel Biltereyst
Brussels, January 2023

Acknowledgements

*E*XPLORING *Cinema Memory* was inspired by a research project, begun in the early 1990s, called Cinema Culture in 1930s Britain: Ethnohistory of a Popular Cultural Practice (CCINTB). Between 1994 and 1996 CCINTB was funded by the United Kingdom Economic and Social Research Council and based and staffed, under my direction, in the Department of Theatre, Film and Television Studies at the University of Glasgow. The main publication arising from that project, *An Everyday Magic: Cinema and Cultural Memory*, appeared in 2002. In the ensuing twenty years, alongside day-to-day academic commitments, I have intermittently continued work on the project: analysing, interpreting and communicating its findings and participating in outreach activities of various kinds. This book is testimony to the work conducted with CCINTB in the two decades following the publication of *An Everyday Magic* and especially to the identification and early exploration of Cinema Culture in 1930s Britain's foremost and most significant 'discovery' – *cinema memory*.

Over these years CCINTB and I have enjoyed support, advice and assistance from numerous colleagues and friends: Anu Koivunen, Bartosz Kazana, Bill Schwarz, Christine N. Brinckmann, Daniel Biltereyst, Francesco Casetti, Gil Toffell, Gwenda Young, Helen Clish, Helen Hanson, Jean Barr, Julia Hallam, Karina Aveyard, Kate Egan, Les Back, Marc Furstenau, Melvyn Stokes, Nick Wadham-Smith, Nirmal Puwar, Pavel Skopal, Philippa Brewster, Philippe Meers, Richard Maltby, Susannah Radstone, Tytti Soila, Veronika Rall, Vinzenz Hediger, Zeenat Saleh, Zoe Druick and many others. I am indebted, too, to my inspiring associates in the Transitional Phenomena and

Cultural Experience Study Group –- Matt Hills, Patricia Townsend, Phyllis Creme, Suzy Gordon, Tania Zittoun and the late and much-missed Amal Treacher Kabesh. Occasional funding and other forms of support during this period were generously extended by the Arts and Humanities Research Council, the British Academy, Lancaster University and the School of Languages, Linguistics and Film at Queen Mary University of London.

Since 2002 hundreds of people have heard about Cinema Culture in 1930s Britain – at conferences, colloquia, seminars, talks, lectures and lecture series, both in the UK and abroad. I am indebted to organisers for invitations to and to participants for kind responses and helpful feedback at events including: Media Times/Historical Times, Goldsmiths University of London (2003); Culture, Memory and Identity, British Council, Delphi, Greece (2003); Popular European Cinema, Stockholm University (2003); Nothing in Common seminar, University of Turku, Finland (2003); University of Pretoria (2004); Centre for Interdisciplinary Gender Studies Annual Lecture, University of Leeds (2005); Social Cinema Scenes, Goldsmiths University of London (2006); The Glow in their Eyes, Ghent , Belgium (2007); Locarno Film Festival (2007); Raphael Samuel History Centre Annual Lecture, Bishopsgate Institute, London (2007); Culture Unbound, Norrköping, Sweden (2008); lecture series at Masaryk University, Brno, Czech Republic (2008); Simon Fraser University, Vancouver (2009); *Orte filmische Wissens* seminar, Ruhr-University, Bochum, Germany (2010); SERCIA, Besançon, France (2010); Memory and Media, Trento, Italy (2010); PRODOC symposium, Universities of Lausanne, Zurich and Lugano, Switzerland (2011); University College London (2012); Annual Conference of the History of Moviegoing, Exhibition and Reception (HoMER) network, Prague, Czech Republic (2013), University of St Andrews (2014); Academia Film Festival, Olomouc, Czech Republic (2014); Cinema Memory and the Community, The Phoenix, Leicester (2016); University of Liverpool (2018); Annual Conference of the HoMER network, Amsterdam, Netherlands (2018); Mining Memory, University College Cork, Ireland (2019); Annual Conference of the HoMER network, Online (2021).

ACKNOWLEDGEMENTS

Cinema Culture in 1930s Britain was an early adopter within the Humanities of computer-assisted data gathering, recording and organisation and fully entered the digital age in 2019 with the launch of Cinema Memory and the Digital Archive: 1930s Britain and Beyond (CMDA), a follow-on research project funded by the UK Arts and Humanities Research Council and involving collaboration between three universities (Queen Mary University of London, the University of Glasgow and Lancaster University) with myself as Co-Investigator and a research team based at Lancaster. It has been a pleasure to embark on CMDA in the company of a new band of co-workers – Annie Nissen, Claire McGann, Hollie Price, Jamie Terrill, Julia McDowell, Liz Fawcett, Michael Dunne, Richard Rushton, Sarah Neely andSuzy Angus – and with the congenial support and encouragement of the project's UK Steering Committee and International Advisory Group.

Exploring Cinema Memory includes versions of several CCINTB post-2002 publications and conference papers. Chapter 2 is an extended version of an article that appeared in *Screen*, vol. 45, no. 2 (2004); chapter 3 is based on a conference keynote delivered at The Glow in Their Eyes: Global Perspectives on Film Cultures, Film Exhibition and Cinema-Going, Ghent University, in 2007, with an earlier version of the chapter published in Richard Maltby, Daniel Biltereyst and Philippe Meers (eds), *Explorations in New Cinema History: Approaches and Case Studies* (Malden, MA: Blackwell, 2011); chapter 4 first appeared in Annette Kuhn (ed.), *Little Madnesses: Winnicott, Transitional Phenomena and Cultural Experience* (London: Bloomsbury, 2013); chapter 5 is based on a conference keynote delivered at Mining Memories: New Explorations in Cinema, Memory and the Past, University College Cork, November 2019; and chapter 6 had its origin in a short paper delivered online at the 2021 Annual Conference of H0MER.

•

Picture credits.
Cover – poster for a public lecture at Simon Fraser University, Vancouver, designed by Laurynas Navidauskas;

page 6 – A children's matinee, origin unknown;
page 26 – Premier Cinema, Manchester: cinematreasures.org/theaters/33461/photos/87680;
page 62 – The Paramount, Glasgow: Thomas McGoran. Participant Artwork. TM-92-009-OA031. Cinema Memory Archive, Lancaster University Library Special Collections;
page 116 – CMDA website: https://www.lancaster.ac.uk/fass/projects/cmda/

•

Last – and decidedly not least – I owe an enormous debt of thanks to every one of the hundreds of 1930s cinemagoers who so generously shared their memories of 'going to the pictures' in interviews, questionnaires, letters and essays. *Exploring Cinema Memory* is respectfully dedicated to them.

Annette Kuhn
January 2023

1. Exploring Cinema Memory: An Introduction

IN the early 1990s the United Kingdom Economic and Social Research Council launched and funded a seminal project, Cinema Culture in 1930s Britain (CCINTB). Its stated objective was to investigate the ways in which films and cinemagoing figured in the daily lives of people throughout the nation in that decade and it sought to situate cinemagoing and fan behaviour in this period within their broader social and cultural contexts.[1] Alongside research in contemporary source materials relating to cinemagoing, a significant element of the project comprised ethnographic memory work with surviving 1930s cinemagoers, gathering first-hand accounts of a generation's youthful cinemagoing habits and experiences.

Over a period of thirty years or more, this memory work has generated, and continues to generate, novel and culturally significant insights concerning the distinctive qualities of cinema memory. This book documents a key trajectory in this enduring project – a shift away from a broadly cultural-historical emphasis towards a focus on cultural memory. The aim here is to place cinema memory under the spotlight, pinpointing what is distinctive and fascinating about this unique variant of cultural memory.[2]

This chapter sets out an overview of the origins of, and of recent and current shifts and trends within, research and scholarship at the interface between historical film audiences, the cinemagoing experience and cultural memory. It introduces the chapters which follow within this frame, reflecting on some of the methodological issues raised by research in these areas and proposing a new direction for future work in the field.[3]

•

The relationship between cinema and memory may be studied as part of the historical study of film reception and cinemagoing as a social practice and thus of how we think about cinema audiences of the past. In film studies, a general attention to the historical study of cinema audiences has been motivated, over a number of decades, by calls from within the discipline for attention to cultural and institutional issues in the study of cinema alongside a rigorous, evidence-based approach to such historical study. This ambition has benefited from input from the cognate disciplines of cultural studies and memory studies and can also trace roots in certain strands of feminist film scholarship.

In the 1980s, for example, a number of feminist scholars documented and explored the appeal of the 1940s Hollywood woman's picture for female audiences of the time, sparking a series of lively debates about the relationship between these films and their intended consumers – the real women who went to see them.[4] Under the influence of cultural studies-based work on television audiences and on the consumption of popular literature aimed at women, this new attention to the female cinemagoer fed into a number of small-scale empirical studies of female cinema audiences, both past and current. Jacqueline Bobo investigated black women's contemporary responses to the film *The Color Purple* (Steven Spielberg, US, 1985); Helen Taylor looked at female fans of *Gone With the Wind* (Victor Fleming, US, 1939); and, drawing on research conducted in the late 1980s, Jackie Stacey documented British women's recollections of seeing Hollywood films during the 1950s.[5]

At the same time a similar shift towards attention to the past reception of films was emerging within film historiography. Published

An Introduction

in 1985, Robert C. Allen and Douglas Gomery's *Film History: Theory and Practice* argued for a rigorous, empirical approach towards research and scholarship in film history and for giving proper attention to the technological, economic, social and aesthetic contexts in which films were produced, distributed, exhibited and consumed.[6] That book sparked a 'revisionist' approach to doing film history, emphasising the importance of systematic archival inquiry involving primary source material relating to films and their social, economic and industrial contexts – as against the emphasis on canonical directors and their masterpieces that had dominated earlier histories of film and cinema. This revisionism has transformed the conduct of film-historical research and scholarship, inspiring fresh approaches to the historical study of Hollywood cinema and eventually provoking a shift of attention away from a dominant focus on Hollywood and its audiences and towards a transnational approach to the subject, while launching New Cinema History, 'an emerging trend in research into cinema history [that] has shifted its focus away from the content of films to consider their circulation and consumption and to examine the cinema as a site of social and cultural exchange'.[7]

It was in this context that I embarked, in the early 1990s, on what has turned out to be an extended historical inquiry into cinemagoing in Britain that began with a small-scale investigation of popular cinema culture in the 1930s.[8] Cinema Culture in 1930s Britain: Ethnohistory of a Popular Cultural Practice (to give it its full title) emerged from this. CCINTB involved, as participants, both male and female cinemagoers located across Britain and its initial findings were published in 2002 in *An Everyday Magic: Cinema and Cultural Memory*.[9] At around the same time a study by Mark Jancovich, Lucy Faire and Sarah Stubbings of the history of cinema culture in the British Midlands city of Nottingham emphasised film consumption and the role of the audience: it involved a mapping of the cultural geography of cinemagoing, with each cinema in the city associated with a specific form of consumption.[10] Beginning in 2005 Daniel Biltereyst, Philippe Meers and their colleagues have led a series of film-historical projects on audiences, programming and exhibition cultures in the Dutch-speaking northern part of Belgium.[11] All these inquiries have been innovative in attempting to reconstruct cinema cultures 'from below', gathering and drawing on informant-generated source materials – the testimonies of cinemagoers themselves, speaking or writing decades after the events being recalled. And although the topic of memory was not an explicit focus for these other investigations, they have by their nature involved memory work.

The term 'ethnohistory' in CCINTB's formal title nods towards a field of inquiry, emerging in the 1940s, whose objective was to document the histories of non-literate societies. Its adoption signalled an intent to deploy oral and other informant-generated accounts as key research resources alongside other kinds of source materials and protocols – popular film magazines of the period in the case of CCINTB, for example – and to take a discursive and context-aware approach to sources and findings. Above all, the aim for CCINTB has been to respect informants as collaborators whilst making no presumptions as to the transparency of their accounts.[12] While all source materials can be treated either as evidence and/or as material for interpretation, the latter is perhaps of particular pertinence when working with first-hand accounts of events and everyday activities of the past: *how* people remember is as much a text to be deciphered as *what* they remember.[13] Cinema memory work involving informants' accounts is productively conducted in tandem with other types of film-historical inquiry, drawing on conventional primary and secondary source materials to delve into histories of, say, exhibition (the places where films are consumed) and programming (what audiences consume). This multi-source strategy potentially opens up fresh perspectives on the physical and institutional contexts of film consumption while also allowing for triangulation of research findings.[14]

In the feminist debates alluded to above, a key point at issue was a concern to distinguish between the idea of women as social beings at the cinema as against the proposition that in their form and content certain types of film embody a 'feminine' or a 'masculine' address or mode of spectatorship. The two entities, the social audience and the implied gendered spectator in the film text, may overlap, of course; but conceptually, and therefore methodologically, speaking they inhabit different worlds. Both the cultural studies focus within film studies and the revisionist turn within film historiography, however, direct the spotlight on the social audience, highlighting how real people experience, or have experienced, or recall having experienced, their filmgoing. The cinema experience, as it is remembered by cinemagoers themselves, is the focus of this book.

Evidence of cinema audiences' experiences may of course be sought from cinemagoers themselves, as in a number of recent initiatives involving audiences for contemporary films. This kind of audience research is a well-established field which typically draws on the methods and protocols of social science- and social psychology-oriented work in communications studies.[15] However, the instrumentality of memory will be increasingly at the forefront the further into the past the experience took place, so that historical audience research that draws on present-day accounts of past cinemagoing – on the remembered cinematic experience, that is – will inevitably be obliged to take into account the workings of memory. In other words, getting at *what* people remember about their past experiences of 'going to the pictures' (and, crucially, *how* they recall these experiences) entails treating memory on an equal footing with the actual cinemagoing and looking at the interaction between the two.

This is by no means to suggest that memory poses a problem or an obstacle for this kind of inquiry. On the contrary: treating informants' memories as both evidence and material for interpretation lies at the very heart of memory work. As a method in auto-ethnography, memory work can be defined as 'an active practice of remembering which takes an inquiring attitude towards the past and its (re)construction through memory'.[16] In historical film audience research, memory work will direct itself to informants' accounts, treating these exactly as (re)constructions of the past through personal and collective memory – as particular instances, that is, of cultural productions that can be treated, drawing on their potential as material for interpretation, as memory *texts*.[17]

•

Early in the data-gathering phase of Cinema Culture in 1930s Britain it became apparent from reading interview transcripts that the informants' recollections display a number of repeated themes and tropes. Characteristic themes include, for example, vivid memories of rowdy, anarchic children's matinees; of strategies for getting into the pictures free of charge or through forms of barter; and of film serials with their agonising weekly 'cliffhangers'.[18] These – and other – repeated topics will of course have been informed by the content of the interview schedule, which called for a number of broad subject areas to be covered during interviews. At the same time, however, the interviewing took a relatively unstructured and deliberately open approach: informants were not discouraged from expanding on their own interests and there was freedom to digress, to skip over some topics, or to talk at length about others.[19] Common elements were observable, too, in how informants framed their stories and expressed themselves – in the discursive qualities of their memory talk, in other words.

Approached inductively, informants' testimonies yield a recurrent and circumscribed body of linked themes and discursive registers: discussed in an early chapter of *An Everyday Magic*, these constitute a foundation for much of CCINTB's later explorations of cinema memory.[20] Especially striking is an insistence on *place*, above all in informants' memories of their earliest cinemagoing. This 'topographical memory talk' is marked by a determination on informants' part to name 'their' places – neighbourhoods, streets, picture houses – positioning these places in memory-maps or psychogeographies.[21] Informants may even appear to mentally reinhabit these childhood places as they speak, so that the remembered landscapes of childhood seem to assume the quality of heterotopias across which cinemas are dotted like beacons in the night and where journeys to the pictures begin and end at home. The prominence and instrumentality of place-memory and its association with remembered time are explored in chapter 2, 'Place and Time in Cinema Memory'.

In chapter 3, 'What To Do With Cinema Memory', the tropes observable in the memory talk of participants in Cinema Culture in 1930s Britain and also in some other studies of past cinemagoing are investigated for what they reveal about the interaction of private and public in cinema memory. Drawing on the findings of these studies, three modes of cinema memory, distinguishable from one another in terms of content and mode of expression, are identified. These range from apparently idiosyncratic inner-world memory-productions, through films and cinema visits that are recollected in the context of everyday life events, to 'social cinema scenes' – cinemagoing experiences remembered entirely as collective or community activities.

Chapter 4, 'Home Is Where We Start From', opens up previously uncharted terrain in the exploration of cinema memory. It looks at how topographical memory – tropes of place, space and, crucially, of movement through space – figures in cinema memory by approaching the question through Object-Relations psychoanalysis. This offers a fresh understanding of the inner-world activity potentially at work in engagements with film and cinema as cultural experiences. It is worth bearing in mind that for those who grew up with cinema in the 1930s habitual journeys to the local picture house (invariably remembered as undertaken on foot) often constituted young children's earliest independent ventures outside the home. Such journeys involve, in recollection, deep 'on-the-ground' familiarity with details of the informants' neighbourhoods and of the locations, in personal psycho-geographies, of familiar picture houses – places that offered both a home away from home and a portal into entirely other worlds. This comes across most clearly in CCINTB informants' recollections of their earliest cinemagoing experiences, shaped as these were by their generation's particular social, cultural and historical circumstances. Taking contextual issues on board highlights the malleability of cinema memory, inviting speculation on the future of this form of cultural memory for those growing up in an age in which media consumption involves a very different relationship with home in relation to the outside world, with independence and with cultural experience.

Revisiting the conclusions of chapter 3, chapter 5, 'From Cinema Culture to Cinema Memory', traces the route through which cinema memory and its cultural instrumentality emerged as a – perhaps *the* – central issue for Cinema Culture in 1930s Britain and follows its shift away from the cultural approach that originally motivated that project. It also traces attendant shifts of focus, conceptualisation and methodology through successive project outputs, substantiating the thinking behind, and the naming of, CCINTB's successor project, Cinema Memory and the Digital Archive.[22]

Finally, chapter 6, 'The Bridge and the Passport: Thoughts on the Remembered Cinematic Experience', sums up Cinema Culture in 1930s Britain's substantive, conceptual and methodological contributions to the historical study of the cinema experience. Drawing together threads in the project's discoveries about cinema memory along with the emergent engagement, mooted in chapter 4, with the psychodynamics of cultural experience, it lays the groundwork for positive new directions in researching and understanding the remembered cinematic experience.

Notes

[1] Part of the original funding application to the ESRC can be viewed at: https://www.lancaster.ac.uk/fass/projects/cmda/wpcontent/uploads/2020/01/OriginalProjectProposal.pdf [accessed 9 August 2022].

[2] The five Chapters that follow this Introduction draw on research and scholarship conducted between 2002 and the late 2010s. Where material has been previously published or presented in lectures, conferences, or seminars, it has been variously revised,

corrected, updated, augmented, or condensed for this volume. CCINTB interviews quoted from were conducted by Valentina Bold.

3 This chapter is indebted to numerous conversations with Daniel Biltereyst and Philippe Meers and especially to our three-way collaboration as co-editors of a special issue of *Memory Studies* on Cinema-going, Film Experience and Memory. See Annette Kuhn, Daniel Biltereyst and Philippe Meers, 'Memories of Cinemagoing and Film Experience: An Introduction', *Memory Studies*, 10/1 (2017): 3-16.

4 Annette Kuhn, *Women's Pictures: Feminism and Cinema*. 2nd ed. (London: Verso, 1994): 197-217; Annette Kuhn, 'Women's Genres', *Screen*, 25/1 (1984): 18-28; Andrea Walsh, *Women's Film and Female Experience* (New York: Praeger, 1984).

5 See Janice Radway, *Reading the Romance: Women, Patriarchy and Popular Literature* (Chapel Hill, NC: University of North Carolina Press, 1984); Ien Ang, *Watching Dallas: Soap Opera and the Melodramatic Imagination* (London: Routledge, 1985); Jacqueline Bobo, '*The Color Purple*: Black Women as Cultural Readers', in Deidre Pribram (ed.) *Female Spectators: Looking at Film and Television* (London: Verso, 1988): 90-109; Jackie Stacey, *Star Gazing: Hollywood Cinema and Female Spectatorship* (London: Routledge, 1994); Helen Taylor, *Scarlett's Women: Gone With the Wind and Its Female Fans* (London: Virago Press, 1989).

6 Robert C. Allen and Douglas Gomery, *Film History: Theory and Practice* (New York: Alfred A. Knopf, 1985); Robert C. Allen, 'From Exhibition to Reception: Reflections on the Audience in Film History', in Annette Kuhn and Jackie Stacey (eds.), *Screen Histories: A Screen Reader* (Oxford: Oxford University Press, 1998): 13-21.

7 For example Melvyn Stokes and Richard Maltby (eds), *American Movie Audiences: From the Turn of the Century to the Early Sound Era* (London: British Film Institute, 1999); Melvyn Stokes and Richard Maltby (eds), *Identifying Hollywood's Audiences: Cultural Identity and the Movies* (London: British Film Institute, 1999); Melvyn Stokes and Richard Maltby (eds) (2001) *Hollywood Spectatorship: Changing Perceptions of Cinema Audiences* (London: British Film Institute, 2001); Richard Maltby and Melvyn Stokes (eds), *Hollywood Abroad: Audiences and Cultural Exchange* (London: British Film Institute, 2007). The quotation is from Richard Maltby, Daniel Biltereyst and Philippe Meers (eds), *Explorations in New Cinema History: Approaches and Case Studies* (Malden, MA: Wiley-Blackwell, 2011), page 3. See also Daniel Biltereyst, 'Film History, Cultural Memory and the Experience of Cinema: A Conversation with Annette Kuhn', in Daniel Biltereyst, Richard Maltby and Philippe Meers (eds), *The Routledge Companion to New Cinema History* (London:

Routledge, 2019): 28-38; Kate Egan, Martin Ian Smith and Jamie Terrill, 'Introduction', *Researching Historical Screen Audiences* (Edinburgh: Edinburgh University Press, 2022): 1-13.

[8] Annette Kuhn, 'Cinema Culture and Femininity in the 1930s', in Christine Gledhill and Gillian Swanson (eds.), *Nationalising Femininity* (Manchester: Manchester University Press, 1996): 177-92.

[9] Annette Kuhn, *An Everyday Magic: Cinema and Cultural Memory* (London: Bloomsbury, 2002). Other publications arising from CCINTB are listed in Appendix 1 and may also be accessed via the project's timeline at https://www.lancaster.ac.uk/fass/projects/cmda/index.php/timeline/ [accessed 16 December 2022].

[10] Mark Jancovich, Lucy Faire and Sarah Stubbings, *The Place of the Audience: Cultural Geographies of Film Consumption* (London: British Film Institute, 2003).

[11] Philippe Meers, Daniel Biltereyst and Lies Van De Vijver, 'Memories, Movies and Cinema-Going: An Oral History Project on Film Culture in Flanders (Belgium)', in Irmbert Schenk, Margrit Tröhler and Yvonne Zimmerman (eds), *Film – Kino – Zuschauer: Filmrezeption/Film – Cinema – Spectator: Film Reception* (Marburg: Schüren, 2010): 319–337; Philippe Meers, Daniel Biltereyst and Lies Van De Vijver, 'Metropolitan vs. Rural Cinemagoing in Flanders, 1925–75'. *Screen* 51/3 (2010): 272–280.

[12] Kuhn, *An Everyday Magic*: 6-7; 240-54.

[13] Kuhn, *An Everyday Magic*: 9-12.

[14] Daniel Biltereyst, Kathryn Lotze and Philippe Meers, 'Triangulation in Historical Audience Research: Reflections and Experiences from a Multi-Methodological Research Project on Cinema Audiences in Flanders', *Participations: Journal of Audience & Reception Studies* 9/2 (2012): 690–715.

[15] See, for example, Martin Barker, 'How Shall We Measure Our Progress? On Paradigms, Metaphors and Meetings in Audience Research', *Television & New Media*, 20/2 (2019): 130–141.

[16] Kuhn, *Women's Pictures*: 157.

[17] Kuhn, *Women's Pictures*: 158-169; Annette Kuhn, 'Memory Texts and Memory Work: Performances of Memory in and with Visual Media', *Memory Studies*, 3/4 (2010): 298-313.

[18] These are documented in Kuhn, *An Everyday Magic*, chapter 3.

[19] See Kuhn, *An Everyday Magic:* 244 for the CCINTB interview schedule.

[20] Kuhn, *An Everyday Magic,* chapter 2, especially pages 9-10.

[21] Chris Philo and Hester Parr, 'Introducing Psychoanalytic Geographies', *Social and Cultural Geography,* 4/3 (2003): 283-93.

[22] See Appendix 2.

The Premier Cinema, Manchester in 1925: 'You go to the Premier. . .'

2. Place and Time in Cinema Memory

As a large-scale historical-ethnographic study of the reception and consumption of cinema in Britain during the interwar years, Cinema Culture in 1930s Britain (CCINTB) involved conducting interviews, sixty years or so on, with surviving 1930s cinemagoers. As such, CCINTB is in significant respects a study of cultural memory. This chapter identifies, names and begins to explore the distinctive features of a subtype of cultural memory, one that engages the remembered experience of cinemagoing – *cinema memory*.[1] The issues that arise from this exercise have a wide historical, cultural and even conceptual, resonance, in particular as regards our understanding of *lived* time, the time of inner life: a time (and this is important) lived collectively as much as individually, a time somewhat incongruent with the linear temporality of historical time. In this sense, we are in the territory of Geoffrey Nowell-Smith's 'history of subjectivities',[2] though my path diverges somewhat from his.

•

> Cinema was a real thrill in those days. Mhm. Yeah. Talking about it I can almost feel how I felt. Yeah. Yeah. [laughs] Mhm. It was wonderful.[3]

The contents and the registers of memory talk are always informed by the contexts of remembering;[4] and for members of the 1930s generation like this CCINTB participant, life stage is a significant component of the storytelling context.

As a generation enters old age, its members will try to fashion meaningful stories from their individual and collective lives, assessing their roles as protagonists in their own life stories and proposing fitting closures to these stories. There is often a sense of urgency in the telling. It feels important, perhaps, that these stories be passed on, put on the record for future generations; there is a hope that one's story might have some lasting value in the world. Often, too, the stories themselves have an elegiac quality: they are a summing up of a life; they deliver a verdict ('It was wonderful'), a farewell. Elegy can sometimes embody a transcendence of its own, as if a particular life story stretches towards a meaning above and beyond the individuality of its narrator.

Cinema holds a special place in the life stories of the 'movie-made'[5] generation of the 1930s. For a few it even figures as a central protagonist, the focus of a quest for meaning in life. For the majority, though, the men and women for whom going to the pictures is remembered as a routine and taken-for-granted part of daily life at one time, memories of cinemagoing are attached above all to memories of the places and the people of youth. These memories are at once pleasurable in the recollection and tinged with feelings of loss. Stories of queues and crowds outside cinemas, of galloping home after watching cowboy films at Saturday matinees, of dancing like Fred Astaire, are testimonies, too, to the losses that come with ageing: loss of the loved ones of childhood and youth, loss of a sense of belonging to a neighbourhood or a peer group, loss of health, energy and physical prowess.

Is there anything distinctive about the memories of the men and women who grew up with cinema in the 1930s? What is the essence of cinema memory for this generation? What would this tell us about the relationship between cinema memory and cultural memory? From the many and varied expressions of cinema memory that emerge from the testimonies of 1930s cinemagoers two broad categories of memory emerge. These I shall call *cinema in the world* and *the world in the cinema*.

•

Cinema in the world describes what 1930s cinemagoers recall about the role cinema played in their own lives at the time, in the worlds of family, friends and neighbourhood and of the routines of school, work and leisure time. These memories are marked above all by an insistence on place; or rather on very particular places, the places of earliest memory. For this generation, the places of earliest memory are exactly the places of the first experiences of cinema.

> **Interviewee:** There was plenty [of cinemas] over here in Cheetham. There was the Banjo when we started. Then they opened the Riviera. A beautiful. . . opened about sixty years ago. And the Riviera. Beautiful cinema. And then I don't know, it seemed to go down. Then there was the Temple higher up. Then there was the Premier. Then there's one facing the Premier. Then there was the Shakespeare. Then there was another one, just down the street.
>
> **Interviewer:** That's about seven or eight.
>
> **Interviewee:** You start at the Banjo.
>
> **Interviewer:** Yeah.
>
> **Interviewee:** You go to the Riviera. You go to the Temple. You go to the Premier. You go to the one facing that one. You go to the Shakespeare then to the one higher up. Seven. Within eh half a mile. Or a mile I should say. In a mile.[6]

Cinemagoers of the 1930s also operate a strong category distinction between the unassuming, cheap, familiar, picture houses of their childhood neighbourhoods and the exotic and luxurious new supercinemas invariably remembered as being much further away from home. In memory, the familiar picture houses figure as extensions of home, as very ordinary and taken-for-granted features of the everyday landscape. They are places to go back to again and again. Supercinemas, on the other hand, are associated with memories of out-of-the-ordinary treats, special occasions and above all with courtship.

All cinemas, though, whether ordinary or special, figure in memory as nodal points, centres of attraction and energy, people magnets dotted across memory-maps of the landscapes of youth. Crowds are always thronging around these places and you always have to queue to get in. Inside, everybody is smoking, regular patrons make a beeline for their favourite seats and there is constant hubbub as people come and go all the time. Mothers bring along infants in arms, children are unruly, usherettes struggle to keep order, commissionaires wield disinfectant sprays and couples snog in the back row, spied on by small boys. Even the most ordinary picture house is associated in memory with plenty and generosity: being treated to sweets by a parent, getting free fruit and comics at the matinee, being given a box of chocolates on a first date, sitting through the programme two or three times over for the price of a single ticket. This picture of energy and abundance may offer a clue to what lies behind the feeling of compulsion to return that surfaces in so many memory-stories, an understanding of what it was that drew people to the cinema and made them keep going back.

And yet memories of superabundance also contain their very opposite; for an equally insistent feature of cinema memory is stories about obstacles in the way of getting to the pictures. Constraint and limitation of one kind or other figure prominently in the memories of this generation. In the context of cinema memory this *topos* takes the form mainly of accounts of various trials and tribulations surrounding getting hold of the cash to pay for admission to the cinema; and also, to a lesser extent, of stories of prohibitions such as familial or official vetoes on cinemagoing in general or on certain films or sorts of films. As in all storytelling, though, obstacles are there to be overcome; and there are many accounts of ingenious, devious – and, in these narrators' versions, invariably successful – ruses for circumventing all the difficulties and getting into the cinema.

Such strategies for getting by (or 'making do')[7] figure, too, in other memories of youthful picturegoing: in recollections of collectively pushing at the limits of acceptable behaviour at rowdy matinees, for instance, or of taking time during the school day or during working hours to try out hairstyles and make-up seen in films – or even to bunk off to the pictures. All these memories share a sense of anarchy, subversion and rebellion against the often baffling constraints imposed by the adult world. In essence, they are stories about individuation, about exploring the world outside home and family. They are about becoming a separate person, about asserting a measure of independence, using the safe space of the local picture house to do so. They also embody a past versus present *topo*s: told as they are from the vantage point of old age, these are stories about rising above hardship and finding ways of enjoying life in harsher times.

They are stories, too, about *time*: the time of cinema in the world is remembered above all in terms of the temporality of repetition and routine in everyday life, of the 'cinemagoing habit', the twice or thrice weekly visit to the pictures as it slotted into one's other ordinary activities.

•

The temporality of cinema in the world conjoins the temporality of **the world in the cinema**; and at the point where the two meet, cinema becomes, in Foucault's sense of the term, a heterotopia: 'a sort of place that lies outside all places and yet is actually localizable'.[8]

The world in the cinema is commonly remembered as (to use a turn of phrase that comes up again and again in informants' testimonies) 'another world'. In memory, this other place emerges as at once radically different from the ordinary and yet at the same time, in Foucault's term, 'localizable' – embedded in the everyday. In the remembered world in the cinema, time too possesses something of this mix of the 'localizable' and the 'outside' that characterises the Foucauldian heterotopia.

> And of course, these were kind of, got people from humdrum life and you know... that's two hours of freedom.[9]

Many 1930s cinemagoers recall the experience of being in the cinema very much as a circumscribed licence, a type of liberty whose built-in limits are – in retrospect at least – recognised, accepted, even delighted in. In the 'two hours of freedom' afforded by a visit to the pictures, the time limit is just as important as the freedom itself. Implicitly or explicitly, the idea, or the sensation, of freedom characterises recollections of the experience of time in the cinema. But this freedom is not remembered as limitless. Rather, it has the slightly paradoxical quality of being at once open-ended and circumscribed. To this extent – that it is both outside normal time and embedded in it – this remembered cinema time may be understood, stretching Foucault, as a heterochronia.

But if the temporalities of cinema in the world and of the world in the cinema are conjoined, the one embodies an order of time radically different from that of the other. In memory, time in the cinema comes across as flexible and/or as cyclical: if 'two hours' represents clock time, the structured and bounded time frame of the outside world, then inside the cinema that slice of time seems to assume a shape all its own.

Their first encounter with continuous programming (a practice of exhibition in which screenings run on from one another, with no separate sittings; audience members could enter the auditorium at any time during the show and remain as long as they wished to) is remembered very vividly by most 1930s cinemagoers; in part, undoubtedly, because of the peculiar delights of the experience of time that it brought about:

> **Interviewee:** But then, I mean, you could sit in and see it three times round if you wanted.
>
> **Interviewer:** And was that still something that you –
>
> **Interviewee:** [laughs]
>
> **Interviewer:** That you did. [laughs]
>
> **Interviewee:** If that was a picture I liked, you know.
>
> **Interviewer:** Yeah.
>
> **Interviewee:** I'd say, oh, I'll see some more of that.[10]
>
> **Interviewee:** When you went in to see a programme, erm, you didn't wait particularly for the programme to begin. You just went in anytime. It could've been halfway through or whatever. And then you sort of sat through the programme and then waited to see the bit that you'd missed. And then sort of went out when you came in.[11]

Continuous programming promotes a relation to the fiction feature film's organisation of narration and of narrative time which goes against the grain of the linearity that characterises both clock time and the order of temporality commonly attributed to the classical Hollywood narrative. Since it was not at all unusual, for example, to begin watching a feature film part way through the story, it was a common facet of the cinemagoing experience from the 1930s until the late 1950s to see the end of a film before seeing its beginning. This mode of spectatorship certainly challenges the concept of the self-contained linear narrative with a beginning, a middle and an end, experienced in that order.

With continuous programming, narrative time and narrative closure are modified; and narrative time and viewing time are potentially thrown out of alignment. This, in combination with the opportunity afforded by continuous programming to stay in the cinema for hours on end, watching the same programme several times over, imbues recollections of cinema time with a quality of expansiveness and circularity. And yet cinema time is always remembered within the frame of the temporality of the outside world, a temporality which would always eventually reassert itself. One Glasgow informant tells an amusing story about her earliest visit to the pictures, when she learned the difference between time in the cinema and time outside:

> I was told I could go and it was *The Four Sons*. [laughs] And we went, I went to the cinema on my own and I was allowed to go to the first showing at 2 o'clock. And I went with a friend to the first showing and in these days you just sat right on. There was no change of, no going out. You just went any, in the middle, or any time you walked in, if you paid your fare. So at the end of that my friend said, 'I have to go, Helen.' [. . .] I said, 'I think I'll watch it again.' So I sat on and watched it again and I got out, got up to come out and was passing a friend with her parents and she said, 'Aw, come on, sit beside me. Don't go out, Helen. Just sit with me.' [laughs] So I sat through it again! And at the end of it her parents were going and she said to her parents, 'Could I sit through this again?' and they said 'Well, if Helen'll stay.' [laughs] I sat through that film four times. [laughing] And it was a very sad film. It must have been – if I'd saved my tears, I could probably have swum out of that. And when I got out, my father was waiting, absolutely in a terrible state and didn't know what had happened to me. They'd gone round all my friends and looking for me and the people at the cinema said, no they couldn't interrupt the show, they'd just have to wait till I came out. And my dad was, he was so glad to see me, [laughs] he couldn't make up his mind whether to murder me or welcome me. So, my mum welcomed me home but said 'If you ever do that again, you'll never get back to the cinema again!'[12]

In the testimonies of 1930s cinemagoers, cinema time is precisely a heterochronia: recollected experiences of it derive their quality, their texture, from its very difference from the time of the world outside.

Collisions between the two orders of temporality – of cinema in the world and of the world in the cinema – feature prominently in cinema memory. This is true above all, perhaps, of memories of film serials – and more specifically of 'cliffhangers'. In fact, the cliffhangers which closed episodes of serials are almost excessively present in cinema memory. The dreaded caption

>TO BE CONTINUED...

appears to be branded on many 1930s cinemagoers' memories, precisely no doubt because of the shock of the collision it delivered between the time of the world in the cinema and the time of cinema in the world:

> 'Cause you had to go, you see. 'Cause they had a serial on. Every week! Like Buck Rogers or, oh, old cowboy films. And it got to an exciting part, [laughs] and that went off until next week. So of course you had to go.[13]

Recollected experiences of a sense of incompletion, of the painful and frustrating realisation that there was a whole week to wait for the cliffhanger's *dénouement*, are key features of accounts of cinema in the world for this generation. Besides being about the collision between two kinds of experience of time, these memories are about the place of picturegoing in a weekly routine, about the habit – indeed the necessity – of going to the pictures regularly and repeatedly. For in essence talk of 'cliffhangers' puts into words the very experience of a compulsion to repeat: 'you *had* to go, you see'.

> That meant we had to go to the cinema thirteen weeks in succession. But you know, it couldn't come quick enough! See once you come out of the cinema, on a Saturday afternoon? You'd say to yourself, 'I wonder what'll happen next week? I wonder if he'll get out of that mess that he's in.' See?[14]

In cinema memory, the heterotopia and heterochronia that characterise the world in the cinema engage the body and the senses in particular ways. The warmth of the auditorium and the upholstered comfort of the seat lull the body, easing it into a sensuousness and into a voluptuous sense of a time with loosened bounds. And these remembered experiences of body and temporality appear to be of a piece with certain engagements with a further dimension of the world in the cinema – the world on the cinema screen itself.

1930s cinemagoers' earliest encounters with the world on the screen are often remembered as strange, even terrifying. This is perhaps because ways of negotiating the transition between cinema in the world and the world in the cinema had yet to be learned. But if the world in the cinema soon became readable and so lost some of its strangeness, it continued to be experienced as bigger, more perfect, more magical, than the world of daily life outside. Memories of being 'carried away', of feeling oneself becoming part of the world on the screen; memories of merging with the world in the cinema, even of experiencing a temporary ecstasy, a loss of self sometimes expressed in terms similar to that of the rapture of being in love, may certainly be understood in this light (see chapter 6).

•

These tropes of cinema memory – the insistence on the places of cinema in the world and the conjunction of, and the collision between, everyday time and place and cinema's times and places, assume expression in distinctive registers of memory discourse. Most strikingly, perhaps, memories of the earliest visits to the cinema often have about them a quality of the mythic or the legendary. In the recurrence and precision with which the landscapes of early cinemagoing are laid out in memory talk, for instance, or in the often formulaic character of stories about repeated Odyssey-like journeys from home to picture house and back again, a collective imagination appears to be at work. These memory-stories, experienced and presented as personal, are tapping into a vein of shared cultural memory.[15]

For example, stories so repeatedly told about jam jars substituting for pocket money, about anarchy ruling in the child's domain of the matinee, about vivid nightmarish visions inspired by scenes in films, may well be anchored in a particular time and place for their narrators.[16] And yet in their essentials they have much in common with childhood experiences across the generations. At some level these stories are about the challenges that face every child as it grows up: of becoming a separate person, of testing the waters of the world outside home and family, of coming to terms with the fears and the prohibitions – as well as the attractions – surrounding any venture into the unknown.

Also peculiar to cinema memory is a certain inscription of the body; for example, in stories involving recollections, and even relivings, of bodily sensations and movements. Stories of movement: walking to the cinema, cowering under the seat, dancing along the pavement after seeing a Fred and Ginger film. Stories of sensation: the smell of disinfectant pervading the local 'fleapit'; the imagined feel against the skin of the beautiful clothes worn by film stars, perhaps, or the remembered sensation of wearing a much-loved garment of one's own that was copied from, or inspired by, the pictures; a glimpse on the cinema screen of a briefly exposed leg or shoulder; even the regressive pleasures of feeling oneself cradled in darkness in the depths of a cinema seat.

In these memory stories, narration itself sometimes assumes an embodied character. An interviewee's particular choice of words, or a manner of speaking, perhaps, will suggest movement or sensation. Or the telling itself may be somatised, expressed through the narrator's body in a smoothing of the hair, say, or a hand gesture denoting a gallop, or even in a few dance steps or bars of song. It is as if the memory inhabits the body and can be relived, retold, without recourse to words; or indeed as if the world in the cinema could, and even still can be, carried into cinema in the world via the body. For the 1930s generation, cinema supplies both the contents and the forms of such embodied remembering.

Memories both of the world in the cinema and of cinema in the world engage the body and the senses. And yet at the same time embodied modes of remembering exceed cinema and cinema memory, assuming a far wider purchase within cultural memory.

•

The place where memories of cinema in the world and memories of the world in cinema meet provides a useful point of departure for an inquiry into the particular meanings of cinemagoing for the 1930s generation and more generally for a quest for insight into the relationship between cinema memory and cultural memory in their organisation of place, time and the body. So, memories of the earliest visits to the cinema, of the seductions of the continuous programme and, above all perhaps, of the 'cliffhangers' of film serials, reveal a great deal about how the experience of time inside and outside the cinema structures the experience of time in the collective memory of the 'movie-made' generation.

And the world in the cinema of magnitude, abundance and perfection also has its equivalent in the remembered world outside: diffuse yearnings for the 'lovely' world on the cinema screen, for example, hook both into a general desire for life somehow to be better and also into more grounded, gender- or class-specific wishes that opportunities (to be smarter, better-educated, richer, or whatever) had been more plentiful in those days.

In memory talk, these contrasts and contradictions happily coexist, sometimes embracing, containing, completing one another; so that in the meeting between the world in the cinema and cinema in the world, the dreams, desires and wishes become domesticated. There is a kind of assimilation of the magical, and a making magical of the everyday, which may very well be peculiar to cinema memory as a particular form of cultural memory.

Cinemagoers of the 1930s insist that they understood perfectly well the difference between the world in the cinema on the one hand and cinema in the world on the other. And although their testimonies make it clear that 'the pictures' coloured their daily lives in all kinds of ways, the truth of that claim is not in the least vitiated by this fact. For the dreams, desires, emotions and behaviours engaged and inspired by cinema were rooted and lived in the very concrete and local times and places of cinemagoers' daily lives.

Notes

[1] A version of this chapter appeared in *Screen* 45/2 (2004).

[2] Geoffrey Nowell-Smith, 'On History and the Cinema', *Screen*, 31/2 (1990): 160-171. See also Susannah Radstone and Katharine Hodgkin (eds), 'Introduction', in' *Regimes of Memory* (London: Routledge, 2003): 15; and essays in that volume by Bill Schwarz and Karl Figlio.

[3] Beatrice Cooper. Participant interview, Harrow, 7 November 1995. BC-95-208AT002, Cinema Memory Archive, Lancaster University Library Special Collections.

[4] Annette Kuhn, 'A Journey Through Memory', in Susannah Radstone (ed.), *Memory and Methodology* (London: Berg, 2000): 179-196.

[5] The reference is to the title of Henry James Forman's digest of the 1930s Payne Fund studies of the US cinema audience, *Our Movie-Made Children* (New York: MacMillan, 1933).

[6] Rachel Tarsky. Participant interview, Prestwich, Manchester, 6 June 1995. RT-95-184AT001, Cinema Memory Archive, Lancaster University Library Special Collections.

[7] Michel de Certeau, *The Practice of Everyday Life*, trans. Steven Rendall (Berkeley: University of California Press, 1984), chapter 3.

[8] Michel Foucault, 'Other Spaces: The Principles of Heterotopia', *Lotus*, vol.48-49 (1986): 12. On the heterotopian qualities of cinema in the 1930s, see Annette Kuhn, *An Everyday Magic: Cinema and Cultural Memory* (London: Bloomsbury, 2002): chapters 6 and 7.

[9] Arthur Orrell. Participant interview, Manchester, 7 June 1995. AO-95-175AT002, Cinema Memory Archive, Lancaster University Library Special Collections.

[10] Phyllis Bennett. Participant interview, Norwich, 7 November 1995. PB-95-222AT002, Cinema Memory Archive, Lancaster University Library Special Collections.

[11] Eileen Barnett. Participant interview, Harrow, 18 July 1995. EB-95-195AT001, Cinema Memory Archive, Lancaster University Library Special Collections.

[12] Helen Smeaton. Participant interview, Glasgow, 23 January 1995. HS-92-036AT001, Cinema Memory Archive, Lancaster University Library Special Collections.

[13] Phyllis Bennett. Participant interview, Norwich, 27 October 1995. PB-95-222AT001, Cinema Memory Archive, Lancaster University Library Special Collections.

[14] Thomas McGoran. Participant interview, Glasgow, 30 November 1994. TM-92-009AT001, Cinema Memory Archive, Lancaster University Library Special Collections.

[15] On this question, see Alessandro Portelli, 'The Massacre at the Fosse Ardeatine: History, Myth, Ritual and Symbol', in Katharine Hodgkin and Susannah Radstone (eds), *Contested Pasts: The Politics of Memory* (London: Routledge, 2003): 29-41.

[16] For details, see Kuhn, *An Everyday Magic*, chapters 3 and 4.

3. What to do with Cinema Memory

CINEMA memory is about the form as well as the content of the remembered cinema experience. Drawing on the findings of Cinema Culture in 1930s Britain, this chapter develops a typology of cinema memory, looking at how the personal or the private on the one hand, and the collective or the public on the other, intersect in memories of cinemagoing.[1] As generalisations inductively derived from empirical data, the typology will of necessity be informed by the historical and geographical frame to which they relate. Therefore by way of comparison, and perhaps also as a means of methodological triangulation,[2] reference will be made to several other explorations of cinema and memory.

The first of these is a British Film Institute project called 'Screen Dreams', which involved reminiscence work and interviews conducted during the early 2000s at five cine-clubs for elderly people, mostly in the London area and which dealt with memories of cinemagoing over a much longer period than that covered by CCINTB.[3] I shall also touch on two academic investigations of historical cinema audiences that use methods similar to those deployed in CCINTB in gathering cinemagoing memories from other places and other times – 1950s Italy and 1960s Britain.[4] Finally, I shall bring into play the thought-provoking comments of artist and critic Victor Burgin in his book *The Remembered Film*, which in its consideration of remembered fragments of films and their associations provides a valuable alternative perspective to the emphasis on the social in the other projects.[5]

Among the distinctive features of CCINTB is its 'bottom up' approach, the project's starting point being the experiences – in effect the *remembered* experiences – of actual cinemagoers. The memory work part of that project (especially the interviews that were conducted in the 1990s with men and women who were cinemagoers during the 1930s) produces certain repeated themes in recollections of cinemagoing and certain ways of narrating those recollections: ways, in other words, of 'doing' cinema memory. An examination of these and other expressions of cinema memory sheds light on how cinema memory works and in particular on how the private and the public interact in this variant of cultural memory.

Cinema memory, as we shall see, may simply provide material for solitary reverie or daydream. It may also afford material for stories that we share with others – stories about our lives and the times and places we have inhabited together:

> We mainly were all school kids together... mainly because it was cheap and cheerful and the film suited us... I invariably stood in the queue outside until they let us in with Alec, Gladys, Sid, Keithy – all schoolmates and we're still firm mates. In actual fact *I still see four or five of them now – even at my age and that's nice. We often talk about the old pictures.*[6]

> [F]or the Cinema Trevi, where we could enter for free, thanks to the usher who knew us, we arrived there after a long walk [...] *We still remember these moments, when we meet* and we think about how long the walk was and how we did not notice it.[7]

The reveries and the stories may enter wider, more public, domains in the form of writing, artwork and filmmaking (in the case of Victor Burgin, for example; and also – perhaps more familiarly – of film director Terence Davies, one of whose cinemagoing memories is referred to below); as well, of course, as in various kinds of research, including cinema-historical and local-historical inquiry. These reveries, shared stories and cultural productions may differ outwardly from one another, but they also share certain thematic, discursive, formal, or aesthetic attributes. Isolating these will not only enhance our understanding of the cultural instrumentality of cinema memory, but may also inform further research on cinema memory and even perhaps bring an element of predictiveness to such inquiries.

•

From the findings of Cinema Culture in 1930s Britain I have identified three modes or variants of cinema memory. These are, firstly, remembered scenes or images from films (I call these Type A memories); secondly, situated memories of films (Type B memories); and finally, memories of cinemagoing (Type C memories). The empirical evidence suggests that these three forms or variants of cinema memory are not separate or distinct from one another but are more aptly seen as occupying positions along a continuum, with Type A memories at one end and Type C memories at the other. In many actual instances, these memory-types merge or share characteristics.

Some examples of Type A memories:

> A dark night, someone is walking down a narrow stream. I see only feet splashing through water and broken reflections of light from somewhere ahead, where something mysterious and dreadful waits.[8]

> I only went once. And it was a film, a silent film, about the sea. And these waves were . . . uh. . . making this ship roll, it was a sailing ship and I was so frightened I got on the floor and I was hiding my face in my mother's lap. I was scared stiff. I don't know why. It wasn't really frightening, but I was frightened.[9]

Type A is the closest of the three modes to the 'remembered film'

43

in Victor Burgin's sense: he calls his own vivid and detailed earliest memory of a film in the first quotation a 'sequence-image', since he is recalling 'a sequence of such brevity that I might almost be describing a still image.'[10] In terms of content and tone, both these examples have highly distinctive qualities and the fact that they are very early memories is significant, suggesting that their vividness may, at least in part, result from the fact that the child who experienced these moments had not yet learned to negotiate the transition between the world on the screen and the ordinary world.[11] Very few memories of this sort emerged in CCINTB and I have seen none reported in either the British 1960s cinemagoing project or the postwar Italian cinema audiences inquiry;[12] but in terms of the cultural significance of the finding, their intensity more than compensates for their scarcity.

Remembered scenes or images from films are distinctive in three respects, all of them observable in the two examples quoted above. Firstly, the descriptions have a vividness and a visual quality that is almost dreamlike. Asking himself how he can be sure that the memory is from a film, Burgin can only assert 'I just know that it is. Besides, the memory is in black and white.'[13] These are memories of individual, isolated shots, scenes and images from films whose titles are more often than not forgotten or were never known. And yet even if – indeed perhaps because – they are so enigmatic, these images are obviously still resonant, in all their intensity, in informants' consciousness decades after the recollected event. It is clear that in the present moment of telling, the remembered feelings or sensations associated with these memories are in some way being re-experienced.

It is perhaps worth noting that memories of this type may be historically specific in certain respects. For the Cinema Culture in 1930s Britain participants at least, such memories seem to be associated particularly, but not exclusively, with recollections of having been frightened at the cinema at a very early age.[14] A few of them still recollect with a shudder (and not always accurately in every detail) a particular, very brief, moment in the 1933 version of *The Mummy*, which stars Boris Karloff in the title role. Recollecting the moment in the film 'when they opened the lid and it shows him like, you know, he moves his hand', Mancunian interviewee Annie Wright mentions the film by name and, as we shall see, also recollects some of the circumstances in which she saw it.[15] Another CCINTB participant is unable to recall the title of the film but does seem to be referring to the same one: 'He had one where he sort of come out the coffin, you seen the hand coming up and aw... I was in terror with that one.'[16]

Allusions to *The Mummy* (and the more frequent mentions of its star, Boris Karloff) signal a generationally specific aspect of cinema memory which could offer interesting material for further research. In the 1930s, 'horrific' films and their effect on children were the focus of intense public concern in Britain and the many references in CCINTB to being frightened in the cinema indicate that the issues that exercised adults were indeed affecting young cinemagoers.[17] Another group of films that some of the 1930s cinemagoers remember seeing as children are silent films that depict World War I. These include *Battle of the Somme* (1916), *Four Sons* (1928) and *All Quiet on the Western Front* (1930). For this generation too (the median year of birth of CCINTB interviewees is 1922), silent cinema has the quality of something barely remembered; that coincides with, or predates, their earliest recollected visits to the cinema; and that is on the cusp of their own coming to consciousness. Allusions to World War I films also attest to the fascination with the recent (in terms of one's arrival in the world) past, especially recent war, that appears to mark everyday historical consciousness. Other generations will, of course, remember different films or media texts in this intense manner. But we might predict that fascination with the recent past and with the time of one's own arrival in the world or coming to consciousness, will continue to be apparent in cultural texts that are recalled most vividly.[18]

A second noteworthy feature of Type A memories is that the remembered scenes or images are characteristically very brief and are always recalled in isolation from the film's plot, which is not recounted and indeed is never remembered. These memories are not as a rule accompanied by details of the circumstances in which the film was seen. It is as if the remembered scene or image stands out in sharp relief against a background that is absent, or vague and lacking in detail; or else it has been displaced from any attachment to the context in which it was originally experienced.

Victor Burgin's remembered image is an extreme example of this tendency. He notes that he can remember nothing more about the film than the scene or image he describes: 'There is nothing before, nothing after,' he says, 'no other sequence, no plot, no names of characters or actors and no title.' As to the circumstances in which he saw the film, he implies that he would have been in the cinema with his mother: 'my mother sought distraction at the cinema... I became her companion there.'[19] But this is the adult Victor speaking and there is no hint of his mother's presence within the telling of the memory itself. On the other hand, Tessa Amelan's remembered image, a frightening one, is associated with a memory of seeking comfort by burying her face in her mother's lap.

Miss Amelan's story calls attention to a third distinctive aspect of Type A memories: accounts of these remembered scenes or images characteristically re-evoke strong emotions and/or bodily sensations on the narrator's part. Recollections of hiding or covering one's face, or of cowering under the seat, point to an embodied, and possibly pre-verbal, response that has become linked in memory to the image or the scene itself. It is as if the remembered image or scene and the body of the person remembering it are fused together in the moment of recollection and in the feelings that the memory evokes. There is a sense in which the remembered scene or image enfolds the subject – who nevertheless figures at the same time as an observer of the film scene and the scene of memory, in much the way that Freud describes the subject of fantasy creating and also placing himself within a *mise-en-scène* – at once directing the fantasy scenario and helplessly caught up in it.[20]

All this lends support to Victor Burgin's observation that the remembered film, as one instance of our everyday encounters with the environment of media, is analogous to such 'interior' processes as inner speech and involuntary association and that it bears the hallmarks of the primary processes of the 'raw' dream, daydream or fantasy.[21] This, along with the investment in the visual and the fragmentary and non-narrative quality that is also apparent in Type A memories, aligns them with the non-verbal or the pre-verbal and with the PreConscious and the Unconscious. Referring specifically to his own remembered sequence-image, Burgin notes that this memory, which he associates with a 'particular affect' – a sense of apprehension – becomes somehow diminished when put into words, as if the process of articulation takes the shine off the raw, unspoken, unarticulated, memory image. As in the telling of a dream, he suggests, forcing the synchrony of the memory 'into the diachrony of narrative' leads him 'to misrepresent, to transform, to diminish it.'[22] Elsewhere, Burgin mentions the 'brilliance' that surrounds this kind of memory; a word which captures the feeling of effulgence and vividness apparent also in some of the 1930s cinemagoers' remembered scenes. It is perhaps the bodily, primary-process, pre-verbal, 'inner-speech' quality that still attaches to these now verbalised memories that imbues them also with the directness and simplicity of the child's voice: a quality that is certainly apparent in 1930s cinemagoers' accounts of their remembered scenes and images.

The Type A cinema memories described by Victor Burgin and by some of the CCINTB participants operate on the side of the inner world and the phenomenological. Burgin's rich and resonant descriptions of the experience of the remembered film and of remembering films make especially apparent the connection of these memories to psychical or mental processes, with their marks of interior speech and to productions of the Unconscious or the PreConscious.

Intriguingly, these are among the very attributes of cinema spectatorship explored by Christian Metz and others in work on the psychodynamics and metapsychology of cinema.[23] Moreover, looked at discursively – in terms of their rhetoric or address – these Type A memories display many of the formal qualities that distinguish a cultural genre or mode that I have named, in a rather different context, the 'memory text.'[24] These qualities include in particular a non-continuous or non-sequential quality to the narration or telling; a nonspecificity as to time; a fragmentary quality; a sense of synchrony, as if remembered events are somehow pulled out of a linear time frame or refuse to be anchored in 'real' historical time. Memory texts, in short, share the generally imagistic quality of unconscious productions like dreams and fantasies.[25] Significantly, as we have seen, Burgin notes that his own earliest memory of a film is sufficient ('sharply particular', 'brilliant', he says) within itself and yet at the same time it is vague as to everything outside itself.

The commonalities of observation and interpretation that emerge here indicate that if Type A memories operate on the side of the phenomenological or the metapsychological and bear the marks of inner-world processes, they are by no means to be dismissed as purely subjective, personal, or idiosyncratic. There is clearly at some level something shared and even profoundly cultural, about such 'inner-world' productions. At the same time, however, the fragmentary, non-narrative quality of such memories, as well as Burgin's suggestion that there is 'something private' about them that demands they remain untold, may also begin to explain the relative scarcity of recollections of this type in the records of cinema memory.[26]

•

The cultural is rather more evident in the situated cinema memories that characterise Type B, in which films and scenes or images from films are remembered within a context of events in the subject's own life. This is perhaps equivalent to a type of remembered film that Burgin regards as entirely different in timbre from his own enigmatic and mysterious 'sequence-image', in that the former are associated with consciously recollected events in his childhood, recalled 'either in direct relation to a film, or to something that happened shortly after seeing one.'[27] Burgin cites no personal examples of such memories, but expressions of this type of cinema memory are rather more prominent in CCINTB than examples of Type A. However, the detail and the nature of the remembered film and the associated life events vary considerably across different instances, as do the weight given to each and to the relationship between the two.

> Oh, I remember the first film we went to see him [Boris Karloff] in... erm... at The Globe, in – where was it? – Old Trafford, I think it was. And it was *The Mummy*. Well there were benches then, you know, not seats. I don't know whether I'd left school. Probably I'd left school. Anyway, I went to see him. I was sat there, dead quiet. And when they opened the lid and it shows him like, you know and he moves his hand. Well I let out one [bursts out laughing]... I slid along the seat. I was frightened to death![28]

> I must've been five... eh... and seeing, we came in the middle. Films in those days were continuous. You see. And ...erm... I remember going in and it had already... it must've been halfway through. And I remember seeing Janet Gaynor and Charles Farrell in *Seventh Heaven*. I knew it was called *Seventh Heaven*. I remember them going up this spiral staircase. More than that I don't remember.[29]

Annie Wright's story about when she saw *The Mummy* incorporates a vividly remembered image from the film – but this is set within a story of the cinema visit that also contains a considerable amount of scene-setting detail (the name and location of the cinema, a description of its seating arrangements), as well as her own bodily response to the Mummy's stirring into life. Beatrice Cooper's brief but vivid recollection of an image in Borzage's *Seventh Heaven* (1927), which she mentions in both her interviews, lacks the kind of contextual detail observable in Annie Wright's account, while setting the scene in another, rather intriguing, way. Mrs Cooper's allusion to the practice of continuous programming serves to enhance the 'brilliant' quality of her remembered image by making it, in her memory-story, the very first thing that she saw on entering the picture house as a five-year-old.

Another example of this mode of cinema memory, complete with scene-setting details, sets out a kind of originary moment of an obsession with cinema that was ultimately to inspire the speaker's own creative work:

> When I was seven I was taken by my eldest sister to see *Singin' in the Rain*. Sitting in the dark brown, baroque interior of the Odeon, Liverpool watching Gene Kelly dance with an umbrella, I entered for the first time a world of magic: the cinema.[30]

In discursive terms, Type B memories are distinguished by what I call an 'anecdotal' rhetoric, a form of address that typically involves a story narrated in the first person singular about a specific, one-off, event or occasion, a story in which the informant constructs herself or himself as chief protagonist. The narrator, in other words, figures in the account both as the central character in the personal life events narrated and also as observer of (though not usually as an active participant in) the scenes or images on the cinema screen.[31] In CCINTB, anecdotal address is relatively rare across the entire body of participants' memories; but it is a marked, perhaps even an invariable, feature of Type B cinema memories.

In some narrations of these memories, participants deploy a 'weak' variant of the anecdotal to position themselves as central protagonists of life events or remembered film scenes or images that are in all likelihood (with apologies to *Blade Runner*) implants. Implanted memories might originate, for example – with or without acknowledgement on the informant's part – from family stories. Norman MacDonald recounts a story told him by his mother about his unruly behaviour as a small child taken to a screening of *The Kid* (1921).

> I remember Mother telling me that, eh, the manager or someone in charge had [laughs] come along during the course of the performance and he, 'If you don't keep that child from making so much noise, he'll have to be taken away!' [both laugh] And of course I was screaming with laughter at what was going on, on the screen![32]

A similar story is told by Leonard Finegold, who writes that he was taken to see *Snow White and the Seven Dwarfs* in 1938, at the age of three. He mentions the '(green?) witch/stepmother/queen looking out of a frame. I ran out of the cinema. My mother said she didn't catch me for several hundred yards.'[33]

Sometimes informants' 'memories' of seeing film scenes or images have almost certainly entered their stories after the event, as a particular image has acquired cultural iconicity in later years. A number of interviewees, for instance, 'remember' iconic moments in the 1933 *King Kong* and above all the scene in which King Kong sits atop the Empire State Building.[34] In another common manifestation of this phenomenon, 'Screen Dreams' participant Ted remembers the serials at children's cinema matinees:

> And sometimes there would be drama and I can always remember the lady being tied down on the track and the hero coming to rescue her and the music playing. Pearl White I believe.

These memories tend to give themselves away as 'implants' in that in the telling they lack the 'brilliance' of scenes from the truly remembered film.

Describing what he calls a secreted 'memory' of his mother, 'pale and anxious' and pregnant with him, in a bomb shelter during World War II, Victor Burgin alludes to a rather different manifestation of the 'implant' phenomenon. 'This "memory", of course,' he observes, 'is a fantasy with a decor almost certainly derived from a film.'[35] He suggests that 'the tendency for personal history to be mixed with recollections from films and other media productions' is 'almost universal.'[36]

Investigating the same phenomenon, in which recollections of life events become unconsciously coloured or shaped by scenes in films, oral historian Marie-Claude Taranger has called them 'second-hand' memories. When Taranger conducted life-story research with a group of women living in southern France, a number of her informants talked about how, in the absence of nylon stockings during World War II, they improvised by painting seams up the backs of their legs. As

Taranger notes, the details of their descriptions of this activity exactly mirror a scene from François Truffaut's 1980 film set in World War II, *Le Dernier Métro*.[37] At this point, it seems, there is a kind of cultural exchange and recirculation of 'second-hand' memories.

Situated memories tend to lack the 'illumination', the intensity, that mark the remembered scenes or images of Type A. These 'anecdotal' memories bear the traces of having been subjected to various forms of secondary revision; and may well also have been embellished over the years through numerous retellings and by the retrospective addition of details. Unlike the intense and apparently idiosyncratic quality of remembered scenes or images from films, cinemagoing memories of Type B outwardly manifest an active, or at least a potential, social currency as stories that have been shared, negotiated, re-enlivened and even embroidered in retellings over the years.

•

In Type B memories the balance of emphasis in narration between memories of films on the one hand and memories of life events on the other may vary across different instances. Where the balance of emphasis rests mainly on life events, however, Type B memories begin to shade into the third, Type C, mode: memories of cinemagoing.

> Normally when we went to the Ionic, one of us would pay and then having been seated by the usherette would go to the toilet and open the emergency exit doors and let our friends in for free.[38]

> Used to be shelling the nuts on the floor and then they'd take an orange, peel'd be on the floor. All these were going backwards and forwards. There was no peace [. . .] And. . . erm. . . you sit next to some children you could smell camphorated oil. You know, they'd have their chests rubbed with camphorated oil.[39]

Memories of this type do not involve 'remembered *films*' at all.

They are actually memories of the activity of going to the cinema. Even in recollections of the very earliest cinema visits – as for example in Ted's 'Screen Dreams' memory quoted above – the name and the location of the picture house are typically carefully noted and there is very often also some detail about the journey to it and the routes taken. Informants also frequently recollect their cinemagoing companions, as well as what it was like inside the cinema: the decor, the seating, the behaviour of the staff and the audience and so on.

In Cinema Culture in 1930s Britain, Type C memories are more prevalent by far than those in the other two categories; and they are normally recounted entirely separately from memories of actual films. In fact, one of the key conclusions to emerge from the project is that, certainly in the memories of the vast majority of these cinemagoers of the 1930s generation, the essentially social act of 'going to the pictures' is of far greater consequence than the cultural activity of seeing films. This is true also of the 'Screen Dreams' accounts, as well as of the memories of the postwar Italian and the 1960s British cinemagoers. Significantly, however, this 'social' mode of cinema memory plays little or no part in *The Remembered Film*, since, as its title suggests, Victor Burgin's book is about film rather than cinema and his central concern lies with the experience of seeing and remembering films.

Memories of cinemagoing are often discursively marked by the deployment of a 'repetitive' type of narrative rhetoric. In 'repetitive memory discourse' – the stance in fact most frequently adopted by the 1930s cinemagoers – the narrator implicates himself or herself in the events recollected, but (by contrast with the anecdotal) represents those events as habitual rather than as singular or one-off. Often the narrator will adopt the first person plural, which brings with it a certain personal distance from the events being narrated, while at the same time imparting a strong sense of collective involvement. 'We used to' is the characteristic introductory turn of phrase here; and it is implicit in both of the stories from CCINTB quoted above. Although Mr Ryall sets the scene in a particular picture house, his story is about what he and his friends habitually did in order to get in to the cinema without paying. Mrs Casey's story about the behaviour of children at matinees suggests that she was part of the scene as an observer of all the naughtiness; but in referring to her fellow picture-goers as 'they', she distances herself somewhat from the anarchic behaviour. Mr Ryall's setting the scene for his story by mentioning the name of his picture house is an instance of another frequently observable attribute of memories of cinemagoing: it is a very striking feature of cinema memory that place operates both a prompt and a *mise-en-scène* of memory.[40]

The overwhelmingly repetitive and collective rhetoric of memory stories of Type C is typically allied with a set of repeated themes and contents and also with stereotypical turns of phrase in the narration. For example, variations on the theme of 'making do' or evading adult authority, all deploying the same narrative tropes and even turns of phrase – stories of collecting jam jars to pay for admission, anarchic children's matinees, stories about getting adults to 'take them in' to 'A' films – come up again and again in CCINTB participants' cinemagoing memories.[41] There are examples, too, elsewhere:

> So you had to go out on Saturday mornings with a bucket and shovel, shovelling up horse manure because we had all the horse traffic around and selling it for a penny a bucket ... All young boys would be doing it because we'd all go to the cinema... This was the Park Cinema up at Hither Green.[42]

> It used to cost tuppence – two pennies old money and we saw a variation of films such as westerns, comedies, not too serious films. Mainly westerns... I did my Saturday morning pictures at the Broadway, at the bottom of Tanners Hill, right opposite Deptford High Street. That was well used by everyone in my area.[43]

> For a couple of hours or so on a Friday evening we all felt a little closer to the swinging sixties scene. Then it was back home on the bus, elated, with a bit more swagger in our step.[44]

This significant observation draws us onto a little-explored byway in the terrain of oral history studies, where it has been observed that raw oral history interview material, especially from working-class or peasant informants, often features conventional forms of speech and modes of narration in a manner that melds the personal with the collective or frames the personal within a collective experience. As the Italian historian Sandro Portelli notes,

> The degree of presence of 'formalised materials' like proverbs, songs, formulaic language, stereotypes, can be a measure of the degree of presence of a 'collective viewpoint.'[45]

The repeated themes and formulaic modes of telling that mark so many of these memories of cinemagoing, allied with the continuing active currency of these much-told stories, may well signal something that is quite distinctive and culturally significant about this variant of cultural memory – and not only in relation to a single generation or one country. The collective forms and currencies of Type C memories, along with their characteristically formulaic themes and contents, suggest a sliding together of the personal and the collective. It also aligns them on the side of the social (and the cultural) and of the social audience (as against the spectator-in-the-text) and locates them on the terrain of film (and media) as these figure in everyday life. In her study of the cinemagoing habits of postwar immigrants from South Asia to Britain, the sociologist Nirmal Puwar coins the apt term 'social cinema scenes' to describe the sociality (and the place-related nature) of this noteworthy aspect of cultural memory and cinema memory and looks at the instrumentality of social cinema scenes in forging collective identities.[46]

•

The attributes, interrelationships and discursive features of the three modes of cinema memory may be summed up as follows:

	A: Remembered scenes/images	B: Situated memories of films	C: Memories of cinemagoing
Similar concepts	sequence-image		social cinema scenes
Attributes and inter-relationships	phenomenological metapsychological primary process inner world/ interior speech PreConscious, Unconscious	secondary revision social currency	social audience everyday life place
Discursive features	fragmented narration memory-text	anecdotal	collective repetitive formulaic

What can be concluded from this about cinema memory, about the remembered film and indeed about the remembered visit to the cinema? What are the uses of this knowledge? What else might it be useful or important to know and how can we go about finding out? Drawing on empirical data, this exploration brings to light a great deal about the discursive, thematic and experiential features of cinema memory and with it much about what marks out cinema memory as a distinctive subtype of cultural memory.

For example, while cinema memory has qualities that might appear universal, even archetypal, these are expressed through memory-stories and other elements that are historically, geographically and generationally situated or specific. At the same time, features of cinema memory that might at first sight seem merely personal or idiosyncratic will usually, on closer inspection, reveal certain shared or collective attributes. Therefore a deeper understanding of how cinema memory works discursively, rhetorically and experientially can bring to light, concretely, some of the psychical and cultural processes through which the acts of remembering film and remembering cinema can bind us into shared subjectivities. This exploration demonstrates how in the production and operation of cinema memory private and public, personal and collective worlds shade into one another, interweave and work together in a range of different ways. Finally, and coming full circle, all this in turn can offer broader insights into the workings of cultural memory in general, especially with regard to the production and preservation of identities and communities.

Because a similar inductive exercise may be conducted with any corpus of cinemagoing memories, it is entirely possible to test the propositions set out here and also to adjust them for sensitivity to historical, cultural and geographical variation in the expression of cinema memory. In this way, research of the kind described in this chapter may inspire a wider, even perhaps a global, perspective on the very concrete and localised remembered experiences of everyday cinemagoing.

Notes

[1] Based on a keynote lecture at 'The Glow in Their Eyes': Global Perspectives on Film Cultures, Film Exhibition and Cinema-Going. University of Ghent, Belgium, December 2007, an earlier version of this chapter was published in Richard Maltby, Daniel Biltereyst,and Philippe Meers (eds), *Explorations in New Cinema History: Approaches and Case Studies* (Malden, MA: Blackwell, 2011): 85-97.

[2] See Daniel Biltereyst, Kathryn Lotze and Philippe Meers 'Triangulation In Historical Audience Research: Reflections and Experiences from a Multi-Methodological Research Project on Cinema Audiences in Flanders'. *Participations: Journal of Audience & Reception Studies*, 9/2 (2012):690-715.

[3] 'Screen Dreams: Cinemagoing in South East London 1920-60', held at the Age Exchange Reminiscence Centre, September-December 2003.

[4] Daniela Treveri Gennari, Catherine O'Rawe, Danielle Hipkins, Silvia Dibeltulo and Sarah Culhane, *Italian Cinema Audiences: Histories and Memories of Cinema-going in Post-war Italy* (New York: Bloomsbury Academic, 2021); Melvyn Stokes, Matthew Jones and Emma Pett, *Cinema Memories: A People's History of Cinema-Going in 1960s Britain* (London: Bloomsbury, 2022).

[5] Victor Burgin, *The Remembered Film* (London: Reaktion Books, 2004).

[6] Ted, 'Screen Dreams'. Emphasis added.

[7] Interviewee Franca, quoted in Treveri Gennari et al, *Italian Cinema Audiences*: 43-44. Emphasis added.

[8] Burgin, *The Remembered Film*: 16.

[9] Tessa Amelan. Participant interview, Prestwich, Greater Manchester, 29 May 1996. TA-95-183-AT001, Cinema Memory Archive, Lancaster University Library Special Collections.

[10] Burgin, *The Remembered Film*: 15.

[11] See chapter 2 on the permeability of 'the world in the cinema' and 'cinema in the world'; and chapter 6 on the permeability of real and imaginary worlds in the child's mental life.

[12] It is perhaps significant in this regard that the interview schedules

of these projects suggest that informants might not have been specifically asked about their earliest cinemagoing experiences.

[13] Burgin, *The Remembered Film*: 16.

[14] Annette Kuhn, *An Everyday Magic: Cinema and Cultural Memory* (London: Bloomsbury, 2002), chapter 4.

[15] Annie Wright. Participant interview, Manchester, 26 May 1995. AW-95-032AT002, Cinema Memory Archive, Lancaster University Library Special Collections.

[16] Helen Donaghy. Participant interview, Glasgow, 3 March 1995. HC-94-012AT002, Cinema Memory Archive, Lancaster University Library Special Collections.

[17] See Annette Kuhn, 'Children, 'Horrific' Films and Censorship in 1930s Britain,' in Richard Maltby, Melvyn Stokes and Robert C. Allen (eds), *Going to the Movies: Hollywood and the Social Experience of Cinema* (Exeter: Exeter University Press, 2007): 323-332.

[18] For further discussion of this phenomenon, see Annette Kuhn, *Family Secrets: Acts of Memory and Imagination* (London: Verso, 2002), chapter 7.

[19] Burgin, *The Remembered Film*: 16.

[20] On enfolding see Laura U. Marks, *The Skin of the Film: Intercultural Cinema, Embodiment and the Senses* (Durham, NC: Duke University Press, 1999); Sigmund Freud, ' "A Child Is Being Beaten": A Contribution to the Origin of Sexual Perversions,' *The Standard Edition of the Complete Psychological Works of Sigmund Freud XVII*. Trans. and ed. James Strachey (London: Vintage, 2001): 177-204.

[21] Burgin, *The Remembered Film*: 14.

[22] Burgin, *The Remembered Film*: 15.

[23] Christian Metz, *The Imaginary Signifier: Psychoanalysis and the Cinema*. Trans. Celia Britton, Annwyl Williams, Ben Brewster and Alfred Guzzetti (Bloomington, IN: Indiana University Press, 1982).

[24] For a discussion of memory texts, see Kuhn, *Family Secrets*, chapter 8.

[25] Kuhn, *Family Secrets*: 160, 162.

[26] Burgin, *The Remembered Film*: 16.

[27] Burgin, *The Remembered Film*: 17.

[28] Annie Wright. Participant interview, Manchester, 26 May 1995. AW-95-032AT002, Cinema Memory Archive, Lancaster University Library Special Collections.

[29] Beatrice Cooper. Participant interview, Harrow, Middlesex, 20 July 1995. BC-95-208AT001, Cinema Memory Archive, Lancaster University Library Special Collections.

[30] Terence Davies, quoted in an exhibition on his work at BFI Southbank, London, March 2007.

[31] Kuhn, *An Everyday Magic*: 10.

[32] Norman MacDonald. Participant interview, Glasgow, 17 November 1994. NM-92-005AT001, Cinema Memory Archive, Lancaster University Library Special Collections.

[33] Leonard Finegold. Participant questionnaire, 30 May 2007. LF-07-008SQ001, Cinema Memory Archive, Lancaster University Library Special Collections. Emphasis added.

[34] Kuhn, *An Everyday Magic*: 77-8.

[35] Burgin, *The Remembered Film*: 15.

[36] Burgin, *The Remembered Film*: 68.

[37] Marie-Claude Taranger, 'Une mémoire de seconde main?' Film, emprunt et référence dans le récit de vie', *Hors-Cadre*, 9 (1991).

[38] J.B. Ryall. Participant letter addressed to Annette Kuhn and Valentina Bold, 8 February 1995. JR-95-48PL001, Cinema Memory Archive, Lancaster University Library Special Collections.

[39] Ellen Casey. Participant interview, Manchester, 31 May 1995. EC-95-182AT001, Cinema Memory Archive, Lancaster University Library Special Collections.

[40] This is touched on in Kuhn, *An Everyday Magic*, chapter 2; and further explored in chapter 2 of the present volume.

[41] Kuhn, *An Everyday Magic*, chapter 3.

[42] Ronald, 'Screen Dreams'.

[43] Ted, 'Screen Dreams'.

[44] Anonymous informant, quoted in Stokes et al, *Cinema Memories*: 9

[45] Alessandro Portelli, 'The Peculiarities of Oral History,' *History Workshop Journal* 12 (1981): 99.

[46] Nirmal Puwar, 'Social Cinema Scenes', *Space and Culture*, vol.10, no.2 (2007): 253-70.

The Paramount, Glasgow: 'Glasgow's premier cinema'

4. Home Is Where We Start From

TAKING a further look at some of the ways in which cinema memory works as a particular type of cultural memory, this chapter proposes that the concepts of transitional object, transitional spaces and transitional phenomena as developed by the pediatrician and Object-Relations psychoanalyst D.W. Winnicott are pertinent and illuminating in this regard, especially as they shed light on the psychodynamics of spatiality. These ideas also have predictive potential, in that they might help us imagine the future of both cultural memory and cinema memory.[1]

The data and the thinking underpinning these propositions come from two separate projects. The first of these is Cinema Culture in 1930s Britain (CCINTB), a study of cinema culture, cinemagoing and cinema memory in Britain in the interwar years which I have been working on since the 1990s. The second is newer work exploring the potential of Winnicottian and other Object-Relations psychoanalysis for extending and deepening our understanding of cultural experience in general and of the cinematic experience in particular. By its nature, the latter project concerns itself both with cinema in its social-institutional sense and with film in its textual, metapsychological, or phenomenological sense.[2] The cinema/film distinction is significant and this chapter concerns itself with the former – with cinema as an institution and with cinemagoing as a social and cultural practice.

Key findings of CCINTB suggest that for the generation that grew up in the 1930s cinemagoing was the occasion for the very earliest ventures into the world beyond the home.

> Close to home, almost an extension of home and yet not home, 'the pictures' is remembered as both daring and safe. Referencing Freud, Michel de Certeau suggests that the back and forth (*fort/da*) movement and the 'being there' (*Dasein*) which characterise spatial practices re-enact the child's separation from the mother. To translate this conceit to cinema memory, it might be argued that, for the 1930s generation, cinema constitutes a transitional object.[3]

The allusion to de Certeau is to his evocative essay 'Walking in the City', in which it is proposed that the everyday 'spatial practice' of walking urban streets is imbued with a particular experience of movement, a 'moving into something different' that repeats 'a decisive and originary experience, that of the child's differentiation from the mother's body'.[4] How was the insight that, for the 1930s generation, cinema constitutes a transitional object arrived at? Why is it important? And what might it suggest about the peculiarities of cinema memory and about the future of cinema memory now that cinema in the form the 1930s generation knew it no longer prevails?

This, above all, is about how place and space figure in certain kinds of memory-stories and about how memory may work through the body, or be embodied. In his phenomenological study of remembering, Edward Casey says that place is important in remembering because it serves to situate one's memorial life in several possible ways. Firstly, Casey suggests, places can act as containers of memory; secondly, places can be *mises-en-scene*, or settings, for remembered events; and thirdly, memory itself is like – or indeed is – a place that we can revisit.[5] Therefore memory both *is* a topography and *has* a topography.

It should be noted that at this point the issue is place rather than the more abstract space. The idea of place suggests attachment – 'being in', belonging – or its absence. Attachment in turn implies a relationship, even a merging of boundaries, between body and place. In the idea of space, movement – movement *in* and movement *through* – arguably figures more pervasively; but figurations of place and space are, as will become apparent, intertwined in the psycho-dynamics of cinema memory.

It was surprising at first to see how insistently place figures in the memories of 1930s cinemagoers. Because this finding is discussed in some detail elsewhere in this volume, however (see chapters 2 and 5), I shall focus mainly on aspects that are of relevance to the current argument. There is a great deal of variation in how place is evoked in cinemagoers' memories and in how metaphors of place organise their memory talk. Nonetheless, emerging from the mix is an overall sense, above all in informants' accounts of their childhood cinemagoing, of a navigation in embodied imagination, even as they speak, of mental topographies of familiar, remembered territory. This topographical memory talk, evoking as it does a psychogeography and a set of spatial practices associated with specific locations, offers important clues as to the ways in which cinema memory works as a distinctive form of cultural memory.

One key finding, for example, is the presence of the discursive 'walking tour' in some informants' accounts of their childhood cinemagoing. This takes the form of a retelling of their route or routes to the picture house, always (implicitly or explicitly) undertaken on foot and often including very precise details of street names and familiar landmarks, recollections of salient features of each cinema and – especially where informants have lived in the same town or city all their lives – information about what currently occupies the sites of cinemas that have been demolished. Such a tour of cinemas in and around Glasgow's city centre is set out in a long letter from John Fowler, a native of the Port Dundas area of the city who had moved away on retirement and was living in Suffolk in the 1990s:

> In our area then the main and I would say biggest was Astoria, in Possil Road, now the County Bingo. One of my memories of the Astoria was the French chocolate nougat,

that they sold. Never, nowhere have I ever tasted any sweets like it, heavenly. Don't remember the admission price, probably 3d or 4d but they always showed the popular films of the time and quite often it was full and there would be standing room, at the back, only. Then they had a waiting room and the patrons were prepared to stand in a long crocodile to see the film, that was changed bi-weekly, not just one but two films. Moving from the Astoria and between it and the Round Toll on the R/H side was the Magnet – this was the bug hutch. It was housed in, I would say the basement part of a slum tenement and the admission was 1d. The projection equipment was suspect and there was frequent breakdowns, this caused the loudest catcalls and feet stamping. Their best of best feature was the serial or 'following up' which always ended at a crucial part and the patrons had to come back next week, to find out.

Next on the tour was the Phoenix, that was down from the Round Toll, towards Cowcaddens. This took us through the slum tenement of Garscube Road, an area of great deprivation. The Phoenix - could be seen from Garscube Road, but was sited in Sawmillfield Street. Never patronised the Phoenix, as it backed onto the canal and had a pungent odour.

Then to Cowcaddens was the 'New Grand', don't know why it was called 'New' possibly it had been rebuilt. This a very nice cinema, though still catering for the poorer masses. I can still picture this, I would call him concierge. He had a lovely uniform, a double-breasted well-tailored uniform, an immaculate white shirt and highly polished shoes, waxed moustache and never wore a cap. On reflection I wonder if he was also the manager. There was an old lady outside, summer and winter selling Seville oranges $1/2$d each. Again, its programme was two films changed bi-weekly.

Round the corner was the Cambridge, almost opposite Stow College. Next to the Cambridge was a bakers called 'Cakeland' this almost as much entertainment as the cinema, as they had a long frontage and one could watch the process from flour to the finished cakes. I can't say for certain on this, but I understood that the Cambridge was the site of Hengler's German Circus. But that was before my time.

Back to travel along Cowcaddens to Hope Street, now here we go upmarket. There was two Gaumont cinemas on Hope Stteet and the other in Sauchiehall Street. One was the Savoy and the other simply the Gaumont. I couldn't afford to frequent these cinemas so I waited till they [films] came to the Astoria or the Grand.

Now opposite in Sauchiehall Street was a very elegant cinema, whose name I can't recall, I only went there once as a special treat. What I do remember is that down the right hand side was a glass screened tea room that was posh. Three-tiered cake stands. We could never afford to use this facility, but I would imagine it was wired for sound, so one could have afternoon tea and watch the film at the same time.

Further along Sauchiehall Street was another cinema, that perhaps was called the Regal, then there was another small cinema near Charing Cross on the right hand side. The next street was Renfield Street and there was the famous Greens Playhouse, which I believe to have been the biggest in Europe. Further down Renfield Street, just below Bath Street, was another cinema, I am not sure, it might have been the Regent. I went there especially to see a film called 'Love on the Dole' whose release had been delayed as it was considered subversive. Didn't think much of it. Further down there was Glasgow's premier Cinema the Paramount, now the Odeon. Then there was a small cinema on the right side, also similar to the one in Jamaica Street.[6]

Mr Fowler's tour is in part a reliving of an embodied childhood memory, in part reminiscence and in part a piece of local history writing.

'Topographical memory talk' has variants, then; but its variants do have certain qualities in common. Firstly, the starting point for the embodied memory-journey is usually the family house, the home, or the home neighbourhood. Secondly, by its nature the journey involves (an imagining of) movement, invariably walking and is goal-directed, its destination being the nearest or next picture house or picture houses. Thirdly, there is a sense of the journey's familiarity, that the speaker or the writer knows (or knew) these streets very well. This is associated, fourthly, with a sense of the journey's ordinariness, its routine quality. Finally, a return home is part of the remembered journey, though this usually remains implicit in the speaker's account.

Underlying the sense of coming and going, of movement away from home or neighbourhood and back again, of the familiarity of the journey's topography, is a sense of *fort/da*, or forth and back, a trying out of separation and independence in a psychical, emotional and physical space of belonging, security, containment. As observed and reported by Freud, the baby's *fort/da* game (repeatedly throwing a cotton reel out of its cot and its mother/carer repeatedly picking it up and giving it back, to the baby's delighted cries of 'Fort!' (gone) and 'Da!' (back)) rehearses presence and absence and models the lesson that objects (including and especially mother) continue to exist even when out of sight.[7] For Object-Relations psychoanalysis the psychical activity at work here figures in specific processes of separation-individuation in which the infant and toddler, in a series of phases lasting until the age of about three, separates itself from the external world and from its mother/primary carer and becomes a separate self – a process, incidentally, that does not stop at the age of three: 'For the more-or-less normal adult, the experience of being fully 'in' and at the same time basically separate from the world "out there" is one of the givens of life that is taken for granted.'[8] For Winnicott, along with the security of a holding environment, the young child's use of the transitional object figures crucially here.[9]

For 1930s cinemagoers, the walk to the local picture house was often the earliest independent venture from home. Home is where these cinemagoers' remembered pedestrian journeys to the cinema start from; and the places and the landmarks named along the way act, in their recollections, like a string that keeps the cinemagoer virtually joined to home, even as they venture away from home and into parts of the outside world that feel familiar and safe, guiding them as they make their way back home. In these memories of being in places and moving through spaces, in other words, the cinema as a place figures as a kind of extension of home. It is significant that these memories invoke a particular sort of cinema building: the neighbourhood picture house, invariably remembered as modest and accessible ('one on every street corner', as a number of informants put it). This is another aspect of their home-like quality (I shall return to the question of different types of cinema). It is also worth pointing out that informants' memories of *going to* the pictures are more numerous and lengthier in the telling than their memories of *being at* the pictures. Going-to and being-at memories also differ markedly in both content and timbre. I shall come back to this point as well.

The observation quoted above – that cinema seemed to constitute a transitional object for the 1930s generation – did not, at the time it was written, feel like a particularly profound insight, nor was it a very considered conclusion. Neither Winnicott nor Object-Relations theory were cited because it never occurred to me to do so. The term transitional object is commonplace in everyday parlance and its usage at this point was undoubtedly imprecise. But this seemingly throwaway allusion somehow set off a new train of thought and a fresh direction for research and the engagement with writings on, and participation in discussions of, transitional objects and culture that ensued have shown that this casual statement contained an idea that was well worth refining and exploring in greater depth.

Transitional objects are the ubiquitous first possessions of infants and young children (perhaps a teddy, or even an old bit of cloth or blanket) that belong at once to the child and its inner world and to the outside world, occupying the place of imagination, an intermediate position between fantasy and reality. Winnicott famously said: 'No human being is free from the strain of relating outer and inner reality',[10] and transitional objects and transitional phenomena help in the negotiation of that relationship. They inhabit what Winnicott called an 'intermediate zone', a 'third area'.

This third area is neither inner psychical reality nor the external world of behaviour and objects, but the space between the two – a bridge, so to speak, that keeps them both apart and joined together. Importantly, transitional objects are material objects, things: they have a physical existence and are pressed into the service of inner reality. They are at once part of the subject and not the subject and in inner life inhabit the intermediate zone, the space between inner and outer worlds.[11]

Winnicott used the term 'transitional space' to refer to the intermediate zone or space inhabited by transitional phenomena. The spatial trope is significant. Winnicott's insights on transitional objects link them largely to childhood and developmental issues, in particular to the activity of playing, whose defining characteristics he regarded as a sense in the child of preoccupation, absorption and near-withdrawal, with the activity itself being experienced as outside the individual and yet not belonging entirely to the external world. Any objects drawn from the external world and used in play are also imbued with the character of inner reality. It is also clear that Winnicott believed that alongside their developmental role, transitional phenomena have a structural aspect as well. In particular, he explored the relationship between transitional phenomena and the ways in which adults experience and relate to culture and creativity.[12] For present purposes, I am interested in exploring both the developmental and the structural aspects of transitional phenomena.

With regard to the former, as noted above, Winnicott linked transitional objects and associated behaviours and psychical processes in infants and young children with issues of separation. This clearly means separation from the mother or primary carer in the first instance but, as Winnicott's dictum 'Home is where we start from' suggests, this extends to include separation from a mother-associated place-object, the *home*.[13] In either case, separation is part of a process of development of self as apart from the outside world and, as described by Winnicott, this process serves as a bridge between the familiar and the unfamiliar and so eases the child's engagement with and acceptance of the new.

It should also be borne in mind that transitional space at once joins objects together and keeps them apart from each other. The structural aspect of transitional phenomena references the fact that the dynamic equilibrium of inner and outer reality is not confined to the transitional objects of childhood but continues through adult life. We continue re-enacting playing and other transitional processes throughout life in relation with our 'adult' transitional objects and phenomena: for the strain of relating outer and inner reality, the task of 'reality acceptance', is never complete.[14]

Place-memory, topographical memory, is pervasive in 1930s cinemagoers' talk, as we have seen and it often manifests itself through tropes of physical movement. As an embodied, kinaesthetic form of memory discourse, place-memory and its invocation of spatial practices re-enacts the interaction of inner and outer worlds that characterises transitional phenomena. And also, through the remembered experience of bodily movement through space in the journeying to and from particular places – in this instance between home and the local picture house – it invokes the rhythms and the repetitions, the ebbs and the flows, of separation processes.

It may not be strictly accurate to state that, for people recollecting and reliving their own filmgoing as children and adolescents in the 1930s the cinema building – the picture house – functions as a transitional *object*. But it can certainly be posited that for this generation the regular comings and goings from home to the familiar neighbourhood picture house and back again partake of the transitional-space activities of relating inner and outer worlds; and that in the particular social and cultural circumstances of their time and place these were part of the separation from home and the exploration of places outside home that are part of growing up.

> As the realisation of the irreconcilability of home and outside space becomes a reality, transitional spaces become a necessity for comfortable functioning. In the outside world these transitional spaces must contain elements of both the mother and world outside: the home away from home, the home on wheels, the freedom to come and go, a place to play.[15]

•

What happens inside the cinema? The remembered walk to the picture house on the street corner is a process of enacting and of restaging one's belonging to a place-object that is outside home and yet like home: one's locality, one's neighbourhood, one's 'manor'. What then takes place inside the cinema is rather different: the virtual experiencing of other, unfamiliar, places. There are in fact two levels involved in the remembered experience of being inside the cinema: being inside the cinema building and in the auditorium on the one hand; and 'being in' (or inside) the world on the screen on the other. Significantly, 1930s cinemagoers' memories of being inside the cinema are far fewer in number and often seem less coherent, than descriptions of the walk from home to the picture house. At the same time, these rare accounts show an exceptionally vivid and emotionally invested quality. They are often also, and perhaps relatedly, unanchored in space and/or time (as in flash-like memories of isolated images or scenes from films, usually frightening or funny ones); or they may be rueful stories about the speaker's failure to understand or properly to negotiate the difference between everyday space and time and space and time in the cinema (see chapter 2). In different ways, all these types of memory are about a difficulty or a lack of proficiency in coping with the illusion/reality relationship; and/or about testing the limits of separation; and/or about managing the transitions from the everyday world to the world of cinema and film and back again.

In these stories, the experience of anticipating the move from the everyday world into the worlds inside the cinema and of the film is remembered above all as straddling the border between different realities:

> I can still remember the excitement of eventually going through the door after waiting in the rain or snow for an hour. That overpowering smell of perfume and – whatever it was, the warmth and the anticipation of going through into the auditorium following the usherette's light, falling over people's feet and settling down in the seat. For 3 hours the outside world was forgotten, worries over school, work, relationships, money disappeared as we lived through the screen.[16]

> Standing in the street queuing in pleasant anticipation of what the next couple of hours had to offer, as the lights dimmed and the screen lit up away we were transported into a world of fantasy.[17]

It is also recalled as involving an involuntary, passive, journey as informants repeatedly talk about being (temporarily) 'transported' or 'carried away': 'It's like being in another world. . . And then when I come out, I'm a bit, you know, kind of ooh! A bit, eh, carried away. And, eh, then I come down to earth eventually.'[18]

It was noted earlier that two very different types of picture house co-exist in 1930s cinemagoers' memories and that the neighbourhood or street-corner type is associated particularly with place-memory, with the 'containing' quality of the home from home and with spatial practices associated with the negotiation of separation-individuation issues. The neighbourhood cinema may thus be regarded as in a sense part of home, or at any rate attached to home. The other sort of cinema, by contrast, is remembered as a place that is wholly separate from the familiar and the everyday. It embodies, in memory, some or all of the following characteristics: it is one of the new 1930s supercinemas, or 'dream palaces'; and it is outside one's neighbourhood – in another town, perhaps, or in the city centre – and is reached not on foot but by mechanised means of transport; it is a place to go to on special occasions rather than as part of a weekly routine; the decor and general ambience of the place are exotic and other-worldly; and it is associated with memories of courtship or romance – that is, with adolescence and adulthood rather than with childhood.

●

These characteristics, I would suggest, have some bearing on how we might imagine the future of cinema memory – by which I mean how (and indeed whether) cinema might figure henceforth in transitional processes, in negotiations of inner and outer realities and processes of separation; and thus how today's – and tomorrow's – cinemagoers and consumers of films might remember these things in years to come. Questions to be addressed in this context could include: Does cinema figure at all today as a transitional phenomenon; and if so, how? How might this involve issues of place and/or space? How might it involve the body? How might the distinction and the relationship between *cinema* and *film* operate today and in the future?

In approaching these questions, it is clearly essential to take into account the impact of changes in the ways in which films and cinema are delivered to the consumer and in how and where films are consumed and used. But it goes beyond this, I believe. Transitional processes are not transhistorical: reality perception and experience of the outer-inner relationship are historically and culturally anchored. It is also worth stating that transitional phenomena, particularly but not exclusively as experienced or remembered in adulthood, can have a collective dimension and so become part of a generational memory bank – as indeed appears to be the case with the memories of cinemagoers of the 1930s.

A number of features of present-day cinema might be regarded as relevant to a discussion about the future of cinema memory. For example, there are far fewer cinema buildings today than there were in the 1930s; in real terms the cost of admission is higher; and the frequency of cinema attendance per capita is much lower now than it was in the 1930s. In short, the public places where one goes to see films today are less available to be experienced as part of the daily routine or of the life of a neighbourhood, or as homes from home. Also, the fact that (certainly in Britain) young children no longer attend cinemas unaccompanied by adults has implications for issues around home and not-home spaces, for spatial practices and for separation-individuation. Because of the element of distance, people of all ages will generally be less likely today to walk to the cinema and more likely to get there by car or public transport. This will surely have implications for the nature of one's attachment' (or lack of it) to the place and to memories of the activity of getting there – to the content, weight and experienced significance of the remembered journey.

Furthermore, there is of course now a wide range of technologies through which films are delivered to and consumed by viewers. For a number of years films old and new have featured regularly in the schedules of broadcast, cable and satellite television, for example. As Roger Silverstone has noted, television texts and even the television set itself may acquire some of the qualities of transitional objects: it is a constant, and constantly available, presence in the home, it possesses some of the qualities of the mother/carer; its schedules and content have a cyclical, routine quality, providing a temporal frame for the viewer and offering a venue for exploring and testing the relations between reality and fantasy.[19] Video, DVD and even streaming permit repeated viewings of films, allowing the viewer to pause, skim and so on: the film text itself consequently becomes a different sort of object – one to be mastered, perhaps, rather than submitted to. We can perhaps surmise that different processes of fantasy, illusion, projection, or introjection may be involved, say, and even that at this point the boundary between cinema as an institution and film as text becomes more permeable.

Today, too, a multitude of forms of entertainment is available and many of these are new. For the 1930s generation, on the other hand, cinema was clearly the main, if not the only, attraction. Cinema is rarely now regarded as cutting edge in the way it was in the 1930s: films and cinema are merely one part of a sprawling and heterogeneous media ecology. In this milieu, new modes of delivery of films and new technologies for their delivery make possible a range of different spatial and bodily relationships with the 'cinematic apparatus' – the physical or the material means of consuming film texts. To the extent that these relationships are potentially more tactile, more immediate, the relationship between films and viewers might in some circumstances become more like that between toys and their users.[20] And yet, to return to Winnicott, we can see that the toy/playing aspect can still potentially involve the kinds of outer world/inner world dynamics at work in transitional phenomena; and that this in turn is likely to impact on future cultural memory. These questions point towards areas of phenomenological and metapsychological inquiry that are ripe for exploration.

The consumption of films and cinema today involves distinctive modes of sociability, relations to places and spatial practices. For example, home media consumption and the attendant organisation of domestic space have implications for the negotiation of separation issues (bedroom culture and so on). On the other hand, going out to see a film in a cinema today is perhaps not unlike 1930s cinemagoers' relationship to cinemas in the second category – those remembered as special, distant, outside the everyday. What will happen to place-memory if the embodied links between home and places outside home are thus transformed, even eroded?[21]

•

This case study, and the questions that it leaves us with, suggests that the Winnicottian concept of transitional space can offer a great deal not only to the student of cultural memory but also to the cultural researcher interested in exploring the interaction between the psychical and the social-cultural, both in general and in relation to the consumption and use of cultural and media texts of different kinds and in different times and places.

Notes

[1] This chapter first appeared in Annette Kuhn (ed.), *Little Madnesses: Winnicott, Transitional Phenomena and Cultural Experience* (London: Bloomsbury, 2013).

[2] Some film-as-text related aspects of transitional phenomena are explored in Annette Kuhn, 'Thresholds: Film as Film and the Aesthetic Experience', *Screen* 46/4 (2005): 401-414; Annette Kuhn, 'Cinematic Experience, Film Space and the Child's World', *Canadian Journal of Film Studies* 19/2 (2010): 82-98; Annette Kuhn, 'Quest Narratives: The Cinematic Experience, Film Space and Transitional Phenomena', *Free Associations* 79 (2020): 77-89.

[3] Annette Kuhn, *An Everyday Magic: Cinema and Cultural Memory* (London: Bloomsbury, 2002): 36.

[4] Michel de Certeau, *The Practice of Everyday Life* (Berkeley, CA: University of California Press, 1984): 109.

[5] Edward Casey, *Remembering: A Phenomenological Study* (Bloomington, IN: Indiana University Press, 1987): 183-4.

[6] John Fowler. Participant letter addressed to Annette Kuhn and Valentina Bold, 13 February 1994. JF-95-153PL001, Cinema Memory Archive, Lancaster University Library Special Collections. The transcription of this letter has deliberately rendered the original text as written, including some spelling and grammatical errors. Some paragraph breaks have been added here.

[7] Sigmund Freud, 'Beyond the Pleasure Principle (1920)', *Pelican Freud Library*, vol.11 (Harmondsworth: Penguin, 1984): 269-338.

[8] Margaret Mahler, *The Selected Papers of Margaret S. Mahler, Vol II: Separation-Individuation* (New York: Jason Aronson, 1979): 131.

[9] D.W. Winnicott, 'Transitional Objects and Transitional Phenomena'. *Playing and Reality* (London: Routledge, 1991): 1-34.

[10] Winnicott, 'Transitional Objects and Transitional Phenomena': 18.

[11] Madeleine Davis and David Wallbridge, *Boundary and Space: An Introduction to the Work of D.W. Winnicott* (London: Karnac, 1990).

[12] D.W. Winnicott, 'The Location of Cultural Experience'. *Playing and Reality* (London: Routledge, 1991): 128-139.

[13] D.W. Winnicott, *Home Is Where We Start From* (Harmondsworth: Penguin, 1986); Anni Bergman, 'From Mother to the World Outside: The Use of Space During the Separation–Individuation Phase', in Simon A. Grolnick and Leonard S. Barkin (eds), *From Fantasy to Reality* (Northvale, NJ: Jason Aronson, 1995): 147-165.

[14] D.W. Winnicott, *Through Paediatrics to Psychoanalysis: Collected Papers* (London: Karnac Books, 2002): 240.

[15] Bergman, 'From Mother to the World Outside': 64.

[16] Margaret Houlgate. Participant letter addressed to Annette Kuhn and Valentina Bold, 20 February 1995. MH-95-111PL001, Cinema Memory Archive, Lancaster University Library Special Collections.

[17] Raymond Aspden. Participant letter addressed to Valentina Bold, [1995]. RA-95-232-PL001, Cinema Memory Archive, Lancaster University Library Special Collections.

[18] Tessa Amelan. Participant interview, Prestwich, Greater Manchester, 28 May 1995. TA-95-183AT001, Cinema Memory Archive, Lancaster University Library Special Collections.

[19] Roger Silverstone, *Television and Everyday Life* (London: Routledge, 1994): 15.

[20] Robert M. Young, 'Transitional'Phenomena: Production and Consumption', in Barry Richards (ed.), *Crises of the Self: Further Essays on Psychoanalysis and Politics* (London: Free Association Books, 1989): 57-72.

[20] On the transformation of cinematic experience in the era of new media, see Francesco Casetti, 'Filmic Experience', *Screen* 50/1 (2009): 56-66; Maria Engberg and Jay David Bolter, 'Mobile Cinematics', in Pepita Hesselberth and Maria Poulaki (eds), *Compact Cinematics: The Moving Image in the Age of Bit-Sized Media* (New York: Bloomsbury, 2017): 165-173.

5. From Cinema Culture to Cinema Memory

AS its official title suggests, the originally intended focus of 'Cinema Culture in 1930s Britain: Ethnohistory of a Popular Cultural Practice' was cultural and historical.[1] And the inquiry did indeed set out with an essentially culturalist approach. Launched with the objective of investigating the ways in which films and cinemagoing figured in the daily lives of people throughout Britain in the 1930s and situating cinemagoing and fan behaviour in this period within their broader social and cultural contexts, the project was in part a response to Jackie Stacey's doctoral study of women's filmgoing in the 1950s. Stacey's inquiry, conducted at the Birmingham Centre for Contemporary Cultural Studies, was later published as *Star Gazing*. Helen Taylor's research on *Gone With the Wind* – the novel and the film – and its female fans, had been published in 1989 and had also been an inspiration.[2] In similar vein, in 1991 I had conducted a small-scale inquiry into popular cinema culture in the 1930s, based upon research in the many British film fan magazines of the period. This fed into a study of cinema culture and femininity.[3]

Stacey and Taylor incorporated questionnaire surveys and other types of informant accounts into their inquiries. Stacey's work emerged from the ethnographic strand of the Birmingham Centre's output, while Taylor's is rooted in the study of US literature and culture.[4] Both were innovative in pursuing inquiries specifically into women as cultural consumers in tandem with a focus on popular culture and in placing women's perspectives front and centre in terms of both substance and methodology. While neither inquiry was rooted in a film studies context, their distinctive approaches have undoubtedly influenced later film studies research into screen audiences of the past.

Cinema Culture in 1930s Britain (CCINTB) attempted to do something new with this ethnographic approach to historical film reception; and besides including men as well as women it aimed to be more self-conscious (and dare I say it, more rigorous) methodologically than the existing work. In this regard CCINTB's research design was guided by the methodological protocols of interpretive sociology, ethnography and oral history. As it turned out, in terms of methodology the project did not draw a great deal from either film studies or cultural studies. The research design was three-pronged, the main emphasis being on an ethnographic-style inquiry among surviving cinemagoers of the 1930s.[5] Arguably one of the most distinctive features of CCINTB is that it yielded data that are at once ethnographically 'thick' and relatively robust in terms of representativeness – data that have therefore been, and remain, qualitatively and interpretively rewarding.

A key – perhaps the principal – element of the ethnographic inquiry took the form of depth interviews with eighty-six surviving 1930s cinemagoers living in four locations in the British mainland: two cities (Glasgow and Greater Manchester), one metropolitan suburb (Harrow in Greater London) and one rural region (East Anglia). The median birth year of interviewees was 1924. Most of the interviews were conducted during 1994 and 1995 and so most of the informants were in their seventies or older at the time. Two questionnaire surveys of self-selected informants were also conducted during the 1990s.

Because transcription of interviews was ongoing throughout 1995 and 1996, it was possible to begin reviewing these materials from early in the life of the project. In some respects, what interviewees recalled (and just as importantly what they did not mention) seemed surprising at first. Informants generally did not talk about individual films very much, or indeed at all. What they did remember most vividly were the places where they went to the pictures in their childhood and adolescence and who they went with. These things were typically recollected alongside other events in their young lives at the time – be it games of Cowboys and Indians played in the street, courtship rituals, or film star-inspired experiments with hairstyles and make-up. Interviewees would talk about stars of the period, usually with some prompting. But they rarely had much to say about particular films featuring their favourites. In other words, interviewees' accounts were focused on cinemagoing as opposed to filmgoing,[6] on cinema culture as part of daily life. These testimonies focus on the social activity of going to the pictures and cinemagoing is typically remembered as part of informants' everyday lives, routines, hobbies and relationships with family and friends. This Mancunian participant's memory is typical:

> [We'd] only got the radio, not the television – every night on the radio there used to be a band from the London, one of the London hotels, so I used to do my home. . . and I can remember this, it always used to be 10:30 at night till midnight, well I would do my homework. By then, I'd been to the pictures, played football and done my homework, 10:30 at night I'm doing my homework till probably one and two in the morning, listening to – well I can't be too sure about these – definitely Lew Stone and his band from the Monseigneur Restaurant on the Wednesday, definitely Roy Fox and his band from the Mayfair Hotel on another night.[7]

The raw substance of such recollections of a lived cinemagoing culture may be called cinemagoing memories, or simply cinema memories. Taken in aggregate, informants' cinema memories display a number of shared substantive and discursive attributes and these are the soil into which the concept of cinema memory seeded itself early in the course of Cinema Culture in 1930s Britain.

For example, the most striking, and perhaps the most intriguing, of these attributes is the centrality and the particular figuration of place and space in the cinema memories. During 1996, the first findings from Cinema Culture in 1930s Britain were reported at a number of conferences at home and abroad. Among these was the *Screen* Studies Conference in Glasgow in the summer of that year. According to the abstract of a plenary lecture entitled 'Place, Space and Cinema Memory':

> Informants are keen to establish precisely where 'their' cinemas were situated, detailing local topographies which link locations of cinemas with other key places in their daily lives. Many recall in vivid detail the process of getting to the cinema and the people they went with. . . In many of these accounts, narrators position themselves within their local topographies, moving freely in the telling from past to present and back again, as well as between remembered places: a sense emerges of narrators navigating mental maps, some of them extremely highly organised, of familiar remembered territory.[8]

Citing examples from CCINTB interviews, the lecture expanded on the instrumentality of place and space in cinema memory and more broadly on the unique qualities of cinema memory as a subtype of cultural memory. This was one of the first public outings for this noteworthy finding. Drawing on CCINTB, the workings of cinema memory have since been explored in greater depth in a number of conference presentations and publications.[9]

In a characteristic instance of the figuration of place in cinema memory, a seventy-nine-year-old interviewee who had lived in Bolton, Greater Manchester from the age of five offers a lengthy discursive tour of the local cinemas that she remembers. In the course of the tour, she 'stops' to tell little stories about some of them:

> You get the main road, St Helen's Road. Eh. . . there was the Rumworth, it was called. And then there was this eh. . . Derby picture house which went to [became] the Tivoli. And that was all along that road. But going over to Deane

Road, there was the Fern Cinema. That's three isn't it, up to now? And then there was the Regent where we used to go. That's four. And then there was a big one. Eh. . . it turned into a skating rink after. And it began with R. It wasn't the Rialto and it wasn't the Regent. But it began with an R. And it was a big cinema that. And they used to say a lot of courting couples used to go there and sit on the back seat, you know. And that was to, I don't know. I never went in, so I don't know. Erm. . . so that was like erm. . . what, one, two, three, four, five. And then there was one on St George's Road called the Rialto. This was called the Imperial. That's six isn't it? There was the Queens on Bradshawgate, that's seven. And then, there was one opened on Bradshawgate erm. . . called the Lido. Now that's still going. I don't know if it's still called the Lido, but it's still going. And I can remember when it was being built. Now I was still at school when that was being built. They used to say, the workmen that were working on it said it would fall down within five-years.[10]

From accounts like this there emerges a sense of navigation of mental topographies of familiar, remembered territory. This 'topographical memory talk' evokes a set of spatial practices associated with very specific places, offering important clues as to some of the ways cinema memory works as a distinctive form of cultural memory. To summarise, topographical memory talk exhibits some or all of the following characteristics: the starting place is home; the journey is on foot and is goal-directed; the journey is oft-repeated; it has a familiar, everyday quality; the return home typically remains implicit.

These and other distinctive discursive features of 1930s cinemagoers' memories are reflected on in a chapter of *An Everyday Magic*, CCINTB's principal publication, that sets out the repeated themes in, and the modes of narrating, recollections of cinemagoing.[11] Some of these are discussed below. Meanwhile, it may be helpful to set out some reflections on how – on the methodology through which – the concept of cinema memory was arrived at. For it is, of course, a concept, an abstraction. But it is an abstraction grounded in empirical observation. It has not been conjured out of thin air but is derived, through a process of induction, from CCINTB interviews and other informant-generated memory materials assembled in the course of the project.

In other words, the concept of cinema memory presents itself in, and arises from, CCINTB's empirical findings. It is not a prior assumption nor is it a hypothesis. Before reviewing the corpus of participants' memory-stories, I had no sense that there could be such a particular thing as cinema memory. To think about this in more concrete terms, you could say that cinema memory is like the essential oil derived from a plant. To start with you might have a sack of tangible stuff: plant materials – leaves, stems, flowers, seeds from a rosemary bush, say. What you end up with is a tiny bottle of essential oil of rosemary. The two things, sack of plant materials and vial of essential oil, are clearly not identical. But they are different aspects or manifestations of the same basic stuff. Some kind of change or transformation has taken place: from the original plant materials oil has been conjured: extracted, reduced, distilled.

This is an analogy, not a scientific explanation – an analogy that can perhaps be pursued a little further. The original plant material may be likened to our 'raw' data – our cinemagoing memories, or cinema memories; and the essential oil to the distillation of these cinema memories to their fundamental features as cinema memory. What is important for present purposes is what has gone on in order to make the raw materials of cinema memories assume their essential form as cinema memory. If this begins to sound somewhat alchemical, it is worth remembering that underlying an apparently magical transformation there lies a procedure – a method, in other words – to both the extraction of essential oils from plants and the inductive identification, from raw empirical data, of a cultural phenomenon, an abstraction, like cinema memory. What, then, are the fundamental features of cinema memory, as they are distilled from the bundles of cinemagoing memories gathered in the course of Cinema Culture in 1930s Britain?

From Cinema Culture to Cinema Memory

•

Three forms or modes of cinema memory, in particular of early or childhood cinema memory, may be identified: firstly, remembered scenes or images from films; secondly, situated memories of films; and thirdly, memories of cinemagoing. The evidence suggests that these three modes of cinema memory are not separate or distinct from each other but are more aptly regarded as occupying positions along a continuum. In particular instances, these may overlap, merge, or share characteristics. Also, since the project is still ongoing, this schema remains a work in progress. These categories may well therefore not exhaust our understanding of the nature and workings of cinema memory. There is always potential for further analysis.[12]

1. Remembered scenes or images from films

> And it was a film, a silent film, about the sea. And these waves were... uh... making this ship roll, it was a sailing ship and I was so frightened I got on the floor and I was hiding my face in my mother's lap. I was scared stiff.[13]

Only a handful of memories like this emerged in Cinema Culture in 1930s Britain, but Victor Burgin recounts a striking one of his own in his book *The Remembered Film*:

> A dark night, someone is walking down a narrow stream. I see only feet splashing through water and broken reflections of light from somewhere ahead, where something mysterious and dreadful waits.[14]

Burgin calls his vivid and detailed earliest memory of a film a 'sequence-image' since he is recalling 'a sequence of such brevity that I might almost be describing a still image'. But in terms of content and feeling tone, both these examples have markedly distinctive qualities and the fact that they are very early memories is key. In terms of the cultural significance of the finding, their intensity arguably more than compensates for their rarity.

Remembered scenes or images from films are distinctive in several respects. They are distinctive first of all in the vividness and the visual quality of the descriptions. These almost dreamlike memories are of individual, isolated shots, scenes and images from films whose titles are forgotten or were never known. And yet these images are obviously still resonant in informants' consciousness, in all their vividness, decades after the event. It seems clear that in the moment of telling *in the present* the remembered feelings or sensations associated with these memories are in some sense being re-experienced.

A second marked feature of memories of this type is that the remembered scenes or images from films are characteristically very brief and are always recalled in isolation from the film's plot, which is not recounted, not remembered. Also, these memories are not as a rule accompanied by any details of the circumstances in which the film was seen: it is as if the remembered scene or image stands out in sharp relief against a background that is absent or blurred and lacking in detail. Victor Burgin's remembered image is an extreme example of this. He notes that he can remember nothing more about the film than the scene or the image that he describes. As to the circumstances in which he saw the film, Burgin implies that he would have been in the cinema with his mother: 'my mother sought distraction at the cinema... I became her companion there'. But this is the adult Victor speaking and there is no hint of his mother's presence within the telling of the memory itself. On the other hand, Tessa Amelan's remembered image, a frightening one, is associated with a memory of seeking comfort by burying her face in her mother's lap.

Miss Amelan's story calls attention to another distinctive aspect of remembered scenes or images: their telling often re-evokes strong remembered emotions or bodily sensations on the narrator's part. Recollections of hiding or covering one's face, or of cowering under the seat, all point to an embodied, pre-verbal, response that has become tied in memory to the image or the scene itself. In relation to all this, it is helpful to look at how the narrator constructs himself or herself in relation to these memories, as well as at the actual content of the memories and how they are narrated. For there is a sense in which the remembered scene or image enfolds the subject – who yet at the same time figures as an *observer* of the film scene and the scene of memory, in much the way Freud describes the subject of fantasy creating, and also placing himself within, a *mise-en-scène*; at once directing the fantasy scenario and helplessly caught up in it.[15]

Referring to his own remembered 'sequence-image', Burgin notes that this memory, which he associates with a 'particular affect' – a sense of apprehension – becomes somehow diminished when put into words, as if the process of articulation takes the *shine* off the unspoken, unarticulated, memory image. Elsewhere he mentions the 'brilliance' that surrounds this kind of memory; a word which captures the feeling of effulgence and vividness apparent also in (some of) the 1930s cinemagoers' remembered scenes. It is perhaps the bodily, primary process, pre-verbal, 'inner-speech' quality that still attaches to these now verbalised memories that imbues them also with the directness and simplicity of the child's voice: a quality that is certainly apparent in 1930s cinemagoers' accounts of their remembered scenes or images.

To sum up, we may infer that the remembered film scenes or images described by Victor Burgin and by a few of the Cinema Culture in 1930s Britain informants operate on the side of the inner world. Burgin's resonant descriptions of the experience of the remembered film (and of remembering films) make especially apparent the connection of these memories to psychical or mental processes, with their marks of interior speech and of productions of the preconscious or the unconscious. Moreover, looked at discursively – in terms of their rhetoric or address – these memories display many of the formal qualities that distinguish a cultural genre or mode that I have elsewhere called the memory text'.[16] These include a non-continuous or non-sequential quality to the telling; a lack of specificity as to time; a fragmentary quality; and a sense of synchrony, as if remembered events are somehow pulled out of a linear time frame or refuse to be anchored in 'real' historical time. Memory texts, in short, share the generally imagistic quality of unconscious productions like dreams and fantasies. Significantly, Burgin notes that his own earliest memory of a film is sufficient ('sharply particular', 'brilliant', he says) within itself and yet at the same time it is vague as to everything outside itself, unspecific as to 'who, where and what'.[17]

The commonalities of observation and interpretation that emerge here indicate that if memories of this kind – remembered scenes or images from films – operate on the side of the phenomenological or the metapsychological and bear the marks of inner-world processes, they are by no means to be dismissed as purely subjective, personal, or idiosyncratic. There is clearly at some level something shared, even deeply cultural, about such 'inner-world' productions. However, the cultural is rather more obviously embedded in the second mode of cinema memory: situated memories of films.

2. Situated memories of films

In memories of this kind, films and scenes/images from films are remembered (or narratively situated) within a context of events in the informant's life.

> There was a Ginger Rogers [film] that I, when I was just not long started working in the Odeon. That's the one in Renfrew Street. The great big one. And I'd gone home for my lunch and coming back from my lunch to go into the office, I worked in... erm... Burns Laird shipping lines, I met this young fellow I knew and he was a student. And he said, 'What are you doing, Helen?' I said 'I'm going back to the office. What are you?' He says, 'I'm going to the pictures to see Ginger Rogers and Fred Astaire.' And I can't remember what it was. One of these singing and dancing... And I said 'Aw!' He said, 'Come on.' And I said, 'Oh, no I can't, no, no, I couldn't. I've got to get back to the office.' He said, 'Oh, look, look who it is. It'll be great.' And I thought, 'Aw, right!' So I went to it. And, oh, I really did enjoy it. I remember it was all singing and dancing and romance and it was just my cup of tea. And when I went home, as we were having

tea, my mum said, 'Where were you this afternoon, Helen?' Oh, crivvens! [laughs] I said, 'I was at work, Mummy.' And she said, 'Now isn't that odd? Your office just phoned to ask what had happened to you.' And that's my lesson for telling lies.[18]

Like the same Glasgow informant's recollection of seeing John Ford's 1928 family saga, *The Four Sons* (quoted in chapter 2), this story emphasises the peer-group sociability and the somewhat transgressive nature of the occasion. The two stories are also of a piece with an intent, voiced throughout both this informant's interviews, to memorialise her mother.

In Cinema Culture in 1930s Britain, expressions of this type of cinema memory are rather more prominent than remembered scenes or images, though the detail and the nature of the remembered film and the associated life events, as well as the weight given to each and the relationship between the two, vary considerably across different instances.

In discursive terms, memories of this type are distinguished by what I term an 'anecdotal' rhetoric, a form of address that typically involves a story narrated in the first-person singular about a singular event or occasion, a story in which the informant constructs herself or himself as chief protagonist.[19] The narrator, in other words, figures in the account both as the central character in the life events narrated and also as observer of these events. In some narrations of these memories, informants deploy what might be called a 'weak' variant of the anecdotal, positioning themselves as central protagonists of life events or remembered film scenes/images that are in all likelihood (with apologies to *Blade Runner*) implants. Implanted memories might originate, for example – with or without acknowledgement on the informant's part – from family stories. For example, while researching the reception of Disney's *Snow White and the Seven Dwarfs*, released in Britain in 1938,[20] I was contacted by Leonard Finegold, who grew up in Hackney, East London. In 1938, at the age of three, he was taken to see the film and still retained a potent memory of 'the (green?) [sic] witch/stepmother/queen looking out of a frame. I ran out of the cinema. My mother said she didn't catch me for several hundred yards.'[21] Sometimes, moreover, informants' 'memories' of seeing film scenes or images have clearly entered their stories after the event – as, for instance, where a particular image has acquired wide cultural currency in later years. For instance, a number of informants 'remember' iconic moments in the 1933 *King Kong*, above all the scene of the giant gorilla perched atop the Empire State Building.[22]

Situated memories tend to lack the 'illumination' – the brilliance, the intensity – that marks the remembered scenes or images of the first mode of cinema memory. These anecdotal memories bear the traces of having been subjected to various forms of secondary revision and they may well also have been embellished over the years through numerous retellings and even by the retrospective addition of details. Unlike the intense, and apparently idiosyncratic, quality of remembered scenes or images, situated memories of films outwardly manifest an active, or at least a potential, social currency. They are stories which are – which have been – exchanged, negotiated, re-enlivened and even embellished in retellings over the years.

As noted, in these memories the balance of emphasis in narration between memories of films on the one hand and memories of life events on the other may vary across different instances. Where the balance of emphasis rests predominantly on life events, this mode of remembering begins to shade into the third type: memories of going to the cinema, or 'social cinema scenes'.

3. 'Social cinema scenes'

> The Ionic was at the far end of the Golders Green and until modernised (sometime after the war, I think) was rather regarded as a flea pit... Normally when I had a few coppers I would go with boys of my own age, occasionally with one of my brothers... The Ionic was the last cinema that I remember taking jam jars in lieu of entrance money...

> Normally when we went to the Ionic, one of us would pay and then having been seated by the usherette would go to the toilet and open the emergency exit doors and let our friends in for free.[23]

Memories of this type do not involve 'remembered *films*' at all. They are actually memories of an activity: going to the cinema. Even when they are recollections of very early visits to 'the pictures', the name and the location of the picture house are often carefully noted and there may be some detail also about the journey to it and of the routes taken. Informants also frequently recollect who their cinemagoing companions were and sometimes also what it was like inside the cinema – the decor, the seating, the behaviour of staff and the audience and even the smells.

In Cinema Culture in 1930s Britain, memories of this kind are the most prevalent by far; and they are normally recounted entirely separately from memories of actual films. In fact, as already noted, one of the key conclusions to emerge from the Cinema Culture in 1930s Britain project is that, certainly in the memories of the vast majority of these cinemagoers of the 1930s generation, the essentially social act of 'going to the pictures' is of far greater consequence than the cultural activity of watching a film. For the project's informants, memories of cinemagoing are discursively marked by the deployment of a 'repetitive' type of narrative rhetoric. In 'repetitive memory discourse' – the stance in fact most commonly adopted by informants – the narrator does not implicate himself or herself in the events recollected, but (by contrast with the anecdotal) those events are represented as habitual rather than as singular or one-off. Often the narrator will adopt the first person plural ('we'), which brings with it a certain personal distance from the events being narrated, while at the same time imparting to the stories a strong sense of collective involvement. 'We used to' is the characteristic introductory turn of phrase here; and it is implicit in the story quoted above. Although Mr Ryall sets the scene in a particular, named picture house, his story is about what he and his friends habitually did in order to get in to the cinema without paying. His setting the scene for his story by mentioning the name and the location of his picture house is an instance of another characteristic attribute of memories of cinemagoing: their investment in place. As already noted, place repeatedly figures in informants' accounts as both a prompt and a *mise-en-scène* of memory.

The overwhelmingly repetitive and collective address of memories of cinemagoing is typically allied with a restricted set of repeated themes, contents and modes of expression. For example, variants of the 'jam jar' theme, references to rowdy children's matinees and memories of getting random adults to help youngsters gain entry to 'A' films abound in informants' cinemagoing memories, which also deploy stereotypical turns of phrase and a circumscribed range of narrative tropes. This resonates with the proposition that raw oral history interview material, especially from working-class or peasant informants, will often feature conventional forms of speech and modes of narration in a manner that melds the personal with the collective, or frames the personal within a collective experience.[24]

The repeated themes and formulaic modes of telling that mark so many of these memories of cinemagoing, especially childhood memories, allied with the continuing and active currency of these much-told stories, seems to signal something significant about cinema memory and in all likelihood not just for a single generation in one country. The collective forms and currencies of memories of cinemagoing, along with their characteristically formulaic themes and contents, suggest a sliding together of the personal and the collective. It also aligns the memories on the side of the social (and the cultural) and of the social audience (as against the spectator-in-the-text as constructed in some branches of film theory) and locates them on the terrain of film and other popular media as these figure in everyday life. In her study of the cinemagoing habits of postwar immigrants from South Asia to Britain, the sociologist Nirmal Puwar has coined the evocative phrase 'social cinema scenes' to describe the sociality (and the place-related nature) of this noteworthy aspect of cultural memory, considering the role of social cinema scenes in forging a sense of collectivity and belonging.[25]

From Cinema Culture to Cinema Memory

•

A close examination of a corpus of cinema memories of members of the 'movie-made' generation of the 1930s, recorded some sixty years after the event, brings to the fore the distinctive features of cinema memory. In the process of distilling the raw data of memories of cinemagoing to the intensified essence of cinema memory, the focus of an inquiry into a past cinema audience shifts away from cultural history and towards cultural memory. At the same time, attention to the most prevalent expression of cinema memory, remembered 'social cinema scenes', signals a return to a consideration of the cultural and the social. Cinemagoing memories constitute the raw materials both for reconstructing a past cinema culture and for uncovering the fundamental features of cinema memory and its instrumentality as a component of cultural memory.

Notes

[1] This chapter is based on a keynote lecture delivered at Mining Memories: New Explorations in Cinema, Memory and the Past, University College Cork, November 2019.

[2] Jackie Stacey, *Star Gazing: Hollywood Cinema and Female Spectatorship* (London: Routledge, 1994); Helen Taylor, *Scarlett's Women: Gone With the Wind and its Female Fans* (London: Virago, 1989).

[3] Annette Kuhn, 'Researching Popular Film Fan Culture in 1930s Britain'. The Reception History of Film and Television, University of Bergen, Norway, June 1992; Annette Kuhn, 'Cinema Culture and Femininity in the 1930s', in Christine Gledhill and Gillian Swanson (eds), *Nationalising Femininity* (Manchester: Manchester University Press, 1996): 177-192.

[4] Such as Paul Willis, *Learning to Labour* (London: Routledge, 2016); Janice Radway, *Reading the Romance* (London: Verso, 1987).

[5] Annette Kuhn, *An Everyday Magic: Cinema and Cultural Memory* (London: Bloomsbury, 2002): 240-254. See also https://www.lancaster.ac.uk/fass/projects/cmda/wp-content/uploads/2022/03/CCINTBResearchDesign.pdf [accessed 19 December 2022].

[6] Jamie Terrill, 'Filmgoing or Cinemagoing? The Role of the Film Text Within Rural Welsh Cinema Memories'. Mining Memories: New Explorations in Cinema, Memory and the Past, University College Cork, November 2019.

[7] Denis Houlston. Participant interview, Levenshulme, Manchester, 26 April 1995. DH95-034-AT001, Cinema Memory Archive, Lancaster University Library Special Collections. For more on Denis Houlston's interviews, see Annette Kuhn, 'Memories of Cinema-going in the 1930s', *Journal of Popular British Cinema*, 2 (1999): 100-120.

[8] Annette Kuhn and Valentina Bold, 'Place, Space and Cinema Memory', *Screen* Studies Conference, University of Glasgow, June 1996.

[9] See Appendix 1.

[10] Freda McFarland. Participant interview, Bolton, Greater Manchester, 7 June 1995. FM-95-189AT001, Cinema Memory Archive, Lancaster University Library Special Collections.

[11] Kuhn, *An Everyday Magic*: 1-12

[12] The discussion which follows reiterates, summarises, and at points expands on, details set out in chapter 3.

[13] Tessa Amelan. Participant interview, Prestwich, Manchester, 29 May 1996. TA-95-183AT002, Cinema Memory Archive, Lancaster University Library Special Collections.

[14] Victor Burgin, *The Remembered Film* (London: Reaktion Books, 2004): 16.

[15] Sigmund Freud, ' "A Child Is Being Beaten": A Contribution to the Origin of Sexual Perversions,' *The Standard Edition of the Complete Psychological Works of Sigmund Freud XVII*. Trans. and ed. James Strachey (London: Vintage, 2001): 177-204.

[16] Annette Kuhn, 'A Journey Through Memory', in Susannah Radstone (ed.), *Memory and Methodology* (Oxford: Berg, 2000): 179-196.

[17] Burgin, *The Remembered Film*: 16.

[18] Helen Smeaton. Participant interview, Glasgow, 23 January 1995. HS-92-036AT001, Cinema Memory Archive, Lancaster University Library Special Collections.

[19] Kuhn, *An Everyday Magic*: 10.

[20] Annette Kuhn, *'Snow White* in the 1930s', *Journal of British Cinema and Television,* 7/2 (2010): 183-199.

[21] Leonard Finegold. Participant questionnaire, 30 May 2007. SW-07-008SQ001, Cinema Memory Archive, Lancaster University Library Special Collections. Emphasis added.

[22] Kuhn, *An Everyday Magic*: 77-78.

[23] J.B. Ryall. Participant letter addressed to Annette Kuhn and Valentina Bold, 8 February 1995. JR-95-048PL001, Cinema Memory Archive, Lancaster University Library Special Collections.

[24] Alessandro Portelli, 'The Peculiarities of Oral History', *History Workshop Journal* 12 (1981).

[25] Nirmal Puwar, 'Social Cinema Scenes', *Space and Culture,* 10/2 (2007): 253-70.

Exploring Cinema Memory

6. The Bridge and the Passport

THIS chapter draws together two approaches to understanding the remembered cinematic experience that have been explored separately in previous chapters.[1] These are: on the one hand cinema memory and on the other the psychodynamics – the mental/psychical engagements – at work in cultural experience. The idea of cinema memory as a distinct variant of cultural memory is derived from the findings of Cinema Culture in 1930s Britain (CCINTB), a research project which involved memory work conducted in the 1990s with cinemagoers of the 1930s. As proposed in chapter 4, the psychodynamics of cinema memory may usefully be understood within the terms of Object-Relations psychoanalysis and the insights it offers on the nature of cultural experience. The objective, then, is to lay the groundwork for a psychosocial approach to understanding the remembered cinematic experience. With this in view, and promising no final answers, this chapter focuses first of all on Object-Relations psychoanalysis and then circles back to the question of cinema memory.

•

My interest in the psychodynamics of cinema memory stems from thinking about how film, as a distinct cultural medium, might mobilise the 'aesthetic moment'. This is a sense of being, or becoming, at one with a work of art. In Object-Relations terms the aesthetic moment entails a sense of mentally crossing over a boundary and entering into another kind of reality – and then returning 'home', renewed: 'an occasion when time becomes space for the subject. We are stopped, held in reverie, to be released, eventually back into time proper'.[2] I first addressed the question of the aesthetic moment in relation to film in 2005,[3] and subsequently convened a study group on Transitional Phenomena and Cultural Experience (T-PACE) with a view to exploring the idea further. The collaborative work of T-PACE, which culminated in 2013 in the publication of *Little Madnesses*,[4] was inspired by the potential of the contributions of pediatrician and child psychoanalyst Donald Winnicott and others in the British Object-Relations School to an understanding of the psychodynamics of cultural experience. ('Little madnesses' is Winnicott's coinage and it refers to our most deeply-felt enthusiasms, investments and attachments in the sphere of culture.) Key terms here include *transitional object, transitional phenomena* and *potential space*.[5]

Transitional objects are the first possessions of infants and young children (a blanket or a teddy, for example) that belong both to the child and to the outside world. Winnicott famously said that no human being is free from the strain of relating outer and inner reality and that transitional objects help with negotiating that relationship. This central idea from Object-Relations psychoanalysis is about the processes through which humans develop and ongoingly manage the contact between the inner world of the psyche and the outer world of objects – in shorthand, the relationship between 'me' and 'not-me'. Transitional objects inhabit what Winnicott called an 'intermediate zone' between inner psychical reality and the external world, keeping the two separate but connected. This *intermediate* space – where 'me' (inner world) and 'not-me' (reality) meet – is the space of playing, illusion, fantasy, creativity and imagination.

The defining features of our engagements with transitional processes may be summarised as follows:

- They are part of the ongoing differentiation between inner and outer worlds, between self and reality;

- They involve a temporary suspension of boundaries between self and objects;

- They 'bridge' inner and outer worlds;

- They involve an oscillation, or a shifting, of boundaries, between inner and outer worlds.

The concept of transitional phenomena stems from Winnicott's 'discovery' of transitional objects, which occupy an intermediate position between fantasy (inner world) and reality (outer world). Importantly, while transitional objects have a material existence, they are also pressed into the service of inner reality. Winnicott used the term 'potential space' to refer to the intermediate zone inhabited by transitional phenomena. For the child, playing resides in this intermediate zone, which is consequently significant in developmental processes. This, according to Winnicott, also grounds all kinds of adult cultural experience, which is located in the potential space between the individual and the environment – a space of maximally intense experiences. To summarise, then: potential space is the intermediate area between 'me' and 'not-me'; it is a 'space between' which partakes of both inner and outer worlds; it is 'the space of illusion, imagination and fantasy'; and it is the space of playing – and of cultural experience.

The point then is what happens where inner and outer worlds meet or conjoin. Here the metaphors of bridge and passport are illuminating as well as evocative. A crucial feature of bridges and passports is that they facilitate activities that can sometimes be tricky or problematic. Besides this they suggest movement or travel, a coming and a going that can be easeful, or possibly not.[6]

This is Winnicott's explanation of cultural experience. He does not greatly expand on this observation, but others in similar Object-Relations vein do – Marion Milner and Gilbert Rose, for instance.[7] But Winnicott's own example of going to a concert and listening to a Beethoven late quartet sums it up neatly enough:

> [W]e go to a concert and I hear a late Beethoven string quartet... This quartet is not just an external fact produced by Beethoven and played by the musicians; and it is not my dream... The experience... enables me to create a glorious fact. I enjoy it because I say I created it, I hallucinated it and it is real and would have been there even if I had been neither conceived of nor conceived.[8]

As cultural psychologist Tania Zittoun notes, 'The quality of cultural experiences *such as listening to a string quartet or watching a film* is obviously "transitional" or "potential": it occurs in the area between inner life and objective reality, demanding elements from each.'[9] In this statement, Object Relations meets cinematic experience, which inhabits the interface of inner ('me') and outer ('not-me') worlds. In other words, Zittoun suggests, an Object-Relations approach can offer an understanding of the specific psychodynamics of the cinematic experience as it works at the border of inner ('me') and outer ('not-me') worlds.

Some nuance may be added to this proposition by asking what, in these (Object-Relations, psychosocial) terms, is particular or distinctive about the cinematic experience as a form of cultural experience. The metaphors of the bridge and the passport are worth looking at more closely here, along with the trope of 'coming and going'. In CCINTB, repeated and consistent expressions around place, space and movement through space are apparent in interviewees' memories of their youthful cinemagoing. There is an especially noticeable insistence on 'coming and going/going and coming' in their memory talk. Aside from the remembered coming and going between home and neighbourhood cinema (see chapter 4), there is also a sense of coming and going between two *topoi* that are at once real places and imaginary spaces. I call these 'cinema in the world' and 'the world in the cinema' (see chapter 2). The former term, cinema in the world, refers to this insistence on the journey made, as a child, from home to familiar local cinema; the latter refers to the world inside the building, the picture house, itself.

The Bridge and the Passport

Early in the course of the Cinema Culture in 1930s Britain project, explorations of 'the world in the cinema' focussed simply on how people talked about memories of being inside a cinema building. Many CCINTB informants, for instance, compare the luxury of a comfortable seat in a warm, carpeted 1930s 'supercinema' auditorium with what was on offer in their more spartan homes. The world in the cinema, however, may also be looked at in terms of the world of the *film*, or the world on the cinema screen. The idea of the film-world, and the cinemagoer's potential interaction or engagement with it, opens up a number of interesting and potentially illuminating avenues of inquiry: for example, looking at the world in the cinema in terms of *filmic* space suggests intriguing possibilities for the conduct of film analysis.[10] The dual meaning of 'the world in the cinema' – the space of both the cinema auditorium and of the world on the cinema screen – is encompassed in a question that was posed, in some form or other, to most of the CCINTB interviewees: 'What did going to the pictures feel like for you in the 1930s?'[11] The appropriate moment for asking this intentionally open question normally presented itself towards the end of the final interview. At this point interviewees appear to have settled themselves into a 'looking back on life' mode and there is a sense in a number of the answers that as they speak, informants are somehow getting themselves inside a kind of *feeling-memory*. Typical responses include the following, taken from interviews conducted across the different CCINTB fieldwork locations:

> **Interviewer:** I mean when you were actually watching the films, did you ever imagine yourself in that sort of. . .
>
> **Interviewee:** Oh when I watched the films, my dear, I was in the picture. 'Cause I thought I was the girl in it [inaudible]. I was wrapped up in it really.[12]

> **Interviewer:** I mean one thing that I did want to ask was, it sounded obviously as if you had a lot of pleasure out of going to the pictures. Erm. . . how did it actually make you feel when you were there? How did you, how did you. . .

Interviewee 1: Really great! You got carried away.

Interviewee 2: Well, yes. That's what I was going to say. Eh . . . you're glued on the screen and eh. . .

Interviewee 1: Yeah

Interviewee 2: That was it. I mean if you were together you didn't have no interest in each other. You were [laughs] glued on the screen.

Interviewee 1: You were absorbed in it.

Interviewee 2: Yeah.[13]

Interviewer: What was it about going to the pictures that you liked so much?

Interviewee: Well, I'll tell you what it was. It's like being in another world. Which it is. And I enjoyed it. And then when I come out, I'm a bit, you know, kind of 'Ooh!' A bit uh, carried away. [laughter] And uh, then I come down to earth, eventually. That's why I like the pictures. Take you out of this world.[14]

Interviewee 1: You know. But. . . erm. . . if you were really enjoying it. . . You did, you did. . . erm. . . you really, yes. . .

Interviewee 2: Mhm yes. Got right into it [. . .]

Interviewer: Did you ever actually imagine yourself in the films?

Interviewee 2: Oh yes!

Interviewee 1: Oh yes!

Interviewee 2: Oh! Particularly Fred Astaire. I used to tap dance all the way home! [laughs] My sister said, 'Stop it!'[15]

Interviewee 1: Our Hilda used to sit there absolutely gone and think [Nelson Eddy] was just singing to her!

Interviewee 2: Well you did!

Interviewee 1: And you know, she was.

Interviewee 2: Yeah, yeah.

Interviewee 1: I used to keep watching her, you know. And when he was smiling she was, as though he was. . .

Interviewee 2: [laughs]

Interviewee 1: Actually smiling at her. Any minute he would come off the screen and she'd be eh. . .[16]

The 'feeling' question, which is essentially about engagements with (in its widest sense) the 'world in the cinema', often elicited conventional turns of phrase – escapism, being carried away, transported to another world and suchlike. However, across the board different sorts of transportation and 'distance' from the everyday world, and varying degrees of intensity of feeling, are articulated. These range from 'losing oneself'; to entering into the film; being 'inside' the film; being called into the film; being addressed personally by a star; and finally to the star 'coming off the screen'.

Many of these expressions embody a sense of the 'aesthetic moment'. In some an impression is conveyed of the cinema screen figuring as a portal through which the cinemagoer can get right inside – and might even feel called or beckoned into – the world of the film. This resonates with the metaphors of the bridge and the passport: the bridge spanning and allowing you to cross over an obstacle or boundary and so enter or be carried to another place or a different world; the passport easing your entry into a different place – with the additional guarantee of facilitating your return 'home'. Indeed returning to your own world is usually implicit (though occasionally quite explicit) in much of this feeling memory-talk. There is evidently more to be considered about the cinemagoer's remembered return from the world in the cinema to the world of the everyday:

> **Interviewer:** I mean, how did you feel when you came out of the cinema? Erm. . . you're saying. . .
>
> **Interviewee:** Oh, you feel refreshed and eh. . . Like eh. . . you know, you've had an experience and you, you know, you went home and you thought, well, I've had a nice night. Enjoyed the cinema and that. And you were ready for work the next day.[17]

This might, perhaps, help in formulating an answer to the question of what, in Object-Relations, psychosocial terms might be distinctive about the cinematic experience as a type of cultural experience.

•

At this point – where Object Relations meets cinematic experience meets cinema memory – we can turn to the question of how an Object-Relations line of thought can shed fresh light on the nature of cinema memory as a variant of cultural memory.

The concept of cinema memory has been developed largely within a New Cinema History frame of reference, in that it derives inductively from empirical research into past cinemagoing.[18] To summarise details set out in chapter 3, three modes of cinema memory are identifiable as emerging in 1930s cinemagoers' accounts:

1. Remembered isolated scenes or images from films.

2. Situated memories of films: films, and scenes or images from films, remembered (or narratively situated) within a context of events in the informant's life.

3. Memories of cinemagoing: memories not of films but of 'going to the pictures'.

These categories may well not exhaust our understanding of the nature and workings of cinema memory: there is always potential for further analysis. And perhaps the Object Relations-resonant qualities of the cinematic experience that seem to emerge in a body of 'feeling-memory' offer exactly this: a locus for further inquiry into cinema memory. In retrospect, the final chapter of the book that came out of CCINTB seems to be groping towards this idea. It is illuminating to return to that chapter with a view to thinking about the psycho-dynamics of the remembered cinematic experience.[19] There it is noted that interviewees' responses to the question of how they felt when watching a film, or after watching a film, embodied three types of 'feeling-memory' response.

Firstly (and in a variant of 'cinema in the world'), there is memory-talk that suggests a down-to-earth, 'of the moment', sense of cinema's place in the daily routines and pastimes of the 1930s:

> But when we did get in [after queuing for ages in the rain], it was always nice and comfortable in most of [the cinemas]. And I think that the warmth and the... eh... kind of comfort. And the plush seats. The darkness and everything. Had a strong, an appeal to us. As the actual films themselves. It was an oasis of comfort and warmth in most of them. Which, in some instances, was even better than our own homes in a way.[20]

Secondly, there is talk that addresses the lived experience of being in the cinema theatre, evoking 'the world in the cinema' and/or indeed the world in the film and (in Object-Relations terms) the potential space of the film-world. A former usherette and chocolate and ice-cream girl recalls:

> As I was standing at the back while Nelson Eddy was singing his love song to me the ice cream used to melt. I danced with Fred Astaire while Ginger Rogers watched.[21]

Thirdly, a number of these reflections touch on potentially wider and deeper meanings of cinema in the informant's life:

> Aw it was great! 'Cause the life, the cinema life then, it was everything! [22]

> But... eh... the cinema was everything to us really. It was to me. And... eh... you could cope with your life.[23]

> **Interviewer:** Did you look forward to going then?
>
> **Interviewee:** Yeah, oh, yeah. Yeah. Yeah, my films were everything to me. Yeah.[24]

For these CCINTB participants, members of a generation that was not on the whole accustomed to articulating deepest feelings, 'everything' appears to connote an all-encompassing and near-inexpressible investment in their cinemagoing. Expressions of this third type of feeling-memory also include intimations that there was something about their cinema experience that made them feel they could be better people, or that held out the offer of 'hope', or 'beauty', or even evoked a kind of transcendence, a yearning for something numinous that did not even have a name, that 'Perhaps one day life will be like that'.[25]

In *Little Madnesses*, the location of cultural experience in the 'potential space' between 'me' and 'not-me' is explored, by means of a case study, in Tania Zittoun's discussion of 'the use of a film' as a symbolic resource for an adolescent; and by C. Lee Harrington and Denise Bielby in an intriguing Winnicottian exploration of cultural experience in later life. Together, their inquiries suggest further valuable ways towards thinking about cinematic experience in the context of the evolving psychodynamics of cultural experience throughout the life course.[26] Meanwhile, the present chapter has ventured some first steps in exploring the place where Object

The Bridge and the Passport

Relations meets cultural experience meets cinematic experience meets cinema memory. This, it is to be hoped, sheds fresh light on the psychodynamics of the remembered cinematic experience.

Notes

[1] This chapter is based upon a paper delivered at the Annual Conference of the History of Moviegoing, Exhibition and Reception Network (HoMER), Online. May 2021.

[2] Christopher Bollas, 'The Aesthetic Moment and the Search for Transformation', in Peter L. Rudnytsky (ed.), *Transitional Objects and Potential Spaces: The Literary Uses of D.W. Winnicott* (New York: Columbia University Press, 1993): 40-49. The quotation is on page 48. See also Marion Milner, 'The Role of Illusion in Symbol Formation', in Rudnytsky, *Transitional Objects and Potential Spaces*: 13-39.

[3] Annette Kuhn, 'Thresholds: Film as Film and the Aesthetic Experience', *Screen*, 46/4 (2005): 401-14. See also Annette Kuhn, *Little Madnesses: Winnicott, Transitional Phenomena and Cultural Experience* (London: Bloomsbury, 2013): 159-166; Daniel Biltereyst, 'Film history, Cultural Memory and the Experience of Cinema: An Interview with Annette Kuhn', in Richard Maltby, Daniel Biltereyst and Philippe Meers (eds), *The Routledge Companion to New Cinema History*. (London: Routledge, 2019): 28-38.

[4] Kuhn (ed.), *Little Madnesses*. Founding T-PACE group members were Suzy Gordon, Matt Hills, Annette Kuhn, Patricia Townsend, Amal Treacher Kabesh and Tania Zittoun. The group was later joined by Phyllis Creme.

[5] D.W. Winnicott, 'Transitional Objects and Transitional Phenomena (1951)', *Playing and Reality* (London: Routledge, 1991): 1-34; 'The Use of an Object and Relating Through Identifications (1968)', *Playing and Reality*: 115-127.

[6] The bridge trope is discussed in Kuhn, *Little Madnesses*, chapter 2. See also Andrea Sabbadini, 'Cameras, Mirrors and the Bridge Space: A Winnicottian Lens on Cinema', *Projections*, 5/1 (2011): 17-30.

[7] See, for example, Marion Milner, 'The Framed Gap', in *The Suppressed Madness of Sane Men* (Hove: Brunner-Routledge 1987): 79-82; Gilbert J. Rose, 'The Creativity of Everyday Life', in

Simon A. Grolnick and Leonard S. Barkin, *Between Reality and Fantasy: Winnicott's Concepts of Transitional Objects and Phenomena* (Northvale, NJ: Jason Aronson, 1995): 347-362.

[8] D.W. Winnicott, 'The Fate of the Transitional Object' (1959), in Clare Winnicott, Ray Shepherd and Madeleine Davis (eds), *Psycho-Analytic Explorations* (London: Karnac Books, 1989): 53-58. The quotation is on pages 57-58.

[9] Tania Zittoun, 'On the Use of a Film: Cultural Experiences as Symbolic Resources', in Kuhn, *Little Madnesses*: 135-147. The quotation is on page 137. Emphasis added.

[10] This is pursued in Annette Kuhn, 'Quest Narratives: The Cinematic Experience, Filmic Space and Transitional Phenomena', *Free Associations*, 79 (2020): 77-89.

[11] The question was added to the interview schedule after the pilot, which was conducted in Glasgow; it had therefore not been put to Glasgow interviewees.

[12] Ethel Cullum. Participant interview, Spixworth, Norfolk, 14 November 1995. EC-95-220AT002, Cinema Memory Archive, Lancaster University Library Special Collections.

[13] Hazel and William Pickess. Participant interview, Lowestoft, Suffolk, 14 November 1995. WP-95-217AT002, Cinema Memory Archive, Lancaster University Library Special Collections.

[14] Tessa Amelan. Participant interview, Prestwich, Greater Manchester, 29 May 1996. TA-95-183AT001, Cinema Memory Archive, Lancaster University Library Special Collections.

[15] Irene and Bernard Letchet. Participant interview, Harrow, 23 November 1995. IL-95-207AT002, Cinema Memory Archive, Lancaster University Library Special Collections.

[16] Vee Entwistle and Dorris Braithwaite. Participant interview, Bolton, Greater Manchester, 5 June 1995. DB-95-038AT002, Cinema Memory Archive, Lancaster University Library Special Collections.

[17] E.J. Godbold. Participant interview, Stowmarket, Suffolk, 27 November 1995. EG-95-214AT002, Cinema Memory Archive, Lancaster University Library Special Collections.

[18] Daniel Biltereyst, 'Film History, Cultural Memory and the Experience of Cinema'.

[19] Annette Kuhn, *An Everyday Magic: Cinema and Cultural Memory* (London: Bloomsbury, 2002): chapter 9.

[20] John Cooper. Participant interview, Bolton, Greater Manchester, 8 May 1995. JC-95-045AT001, Cinema Memory Archive, Lancaster University Library Special Collections.

[21] Isobel Bullock. Participant letter addressed to Annette Kuhn [1995]. IB-95-236PL001, Cinema Memory Archive, Lancaster University Library Special Collections.

[22] Thomas McGoran. Participant interview, Glasgow, 30 November 1994. TM-92-009AT001, Cinema Memory Archive, Lancaster University Library Special Collections.

[23] Doreen Lyell. Participant interview, Lowestoft, Norfolk, 13 November 1995. DL-95-216AT002, Cinema Memory Archive, Lancaster University Library Special Collections.

[24] Phyllis Bennett. Participant interview, Norwich, Norfolk, 17 November 1995. PB-95-222AT002, Cinema Memory Archive, Lancaster University Library Special Collections.

[25] Barbara Harvey. Participant interview, Lowestoft, Norfolk, 18 October 1995. PB-95-215AT001, Cinema Memory Archive, Lancaster University Library Special Collections.

[26] Zittoun, 'On the Use of a Film'; C. Lee Harrington and Denise Bielby, 'Pleasure and Adult Development: Extending Winnicott into Later Life', in Kuhn, *Little Madnesses*: 87-101.

Appendix 1
Cinema Culture in 1930s Britain: Academic Publications

THE LIST which follows is confined to academic outputs (including translations) drawing on the findings of CCINTB and published between 1994 and 2019. Unless otherwise indicated, these are authored by Annette Kuhn.

Along with the items listed here, other pre-2019 outputs (unpublished reports, conference papers, public lectures, radio programmes and so on) are detailed in the CCINTB timeline on the Cinema Memory and the Digital Archive website, where some are available to download: https://www.lancaster.ac.uk/fass/projects/cmda/index.php/timeline/

CCINTB's successor project, Cinema Memory and the Digital Archive: 1930s Britain and Beyond (CMDA), was launched in Summer 2019. Academic and public outputs produced under CMDA's aegis are listed on the project's website, from which a number are available to download: https://www.lancaster.ac.uk/fass/projects/cmda/index.php/outputs-outreach/

1994
'Researching popular film fan culture in 1930s Britain', in J. Gripsrud and K. Skretting (eds), *History of Moving Images:*

Reports from a Norwegian Project. Oslo: Research Council of Norway, 1994.

1996

'Cinema culture and femininity in the 1930s', in Christine Gledhill and Gillian Swanson (eds), *Nationalising Femininity.* Manchester: Manchester University Press, 1996.

'Biografkultur och feminitet i 30-talets England', *Aura: Filmvetenskaplig Tidskrift.* vol.2, no.4 (1996). (Translation by Ylva Habel)

1998

' "Me he acordado de ese día durante toda mi vida": el papel del tiempo y los recuerdos en los fans fieles a una star', *Archivos de la Filmoteca,* no.29 (1998). (Translation by Eva Parrondo Coppel)

1999

'Memories of cinema-going in the 1930s', *Journal of Popular British Cinema,* no.2 (1999).

' "That day *did* last me all my life": cinema memory and enduring fandom', in R. Maltby and M. Stokes (eds), *Identifying Hollywood's Audiences: Cultural Identity and the Movies.* London: British Film Institute, 1999.

'Cinemagoing in Britain in the 1930s: report of a questionnaire survey', *Historical Journal of Film, Radio and Television,* vol.19, no.4 (1999).

Appendix 1 Academic Publications

2000
'Smart girls: growing up with cinema in the 1930s', in Ib Bondebjerg (ed.), *Moving Images, Culture and the Mind.* Luton: University of Luton Press, 2000.

2002
'Children, "horrific" films and censorship in 1930s Britain', *Historical Journal of Film, Radio and Television*, vol.22, no.2 (2002).

An Everyday Magic: Cinema and Cultural Memory. London: Bloomsbury, 2002. Published in the USA as *Dreaming of Fred and Ginger: Cinema and Cultural Memory.* New York: New York University Press, 2002.

2004
'Heterotopia, heterochronia: place and time in cinema memory', *Screen*, vol. 45, no. 2 (2004).

2007
'Children, "horrific" films and censorship in 1930s Britain', in Richard Maltby, Melvyn Stokes and Robert C. Allen (eds), *Going to the Movies: Hollywood and the Social Experience of Cinema.* Exeter: Exeter University Press, 2007.

2009
'Film stars in 1930s Britain: a case study in modernity and femininity', in Tytti Soila (ed.), *Stellar Encounters: Stardom in Popular European Cinema.* London: John Libbey, 2009.

2010

' "I wanted life to be romantic and I wanted to be thin": girls growing up with cinema in the 1930s', in Vicki Callahan and Alison McKee (eds), *Reclaiming the Archive: Feminism and Film History*. Detroit, MI: Wayne State University Press, 2010.

'Was tun mit der Kinoerinnerung?' *Montage AV*, vol.19, no.1 (2010). (Translation by Christine N. Brinckmann)

'Heteropie, Heterochronie: Ort und Zeit der Kinoerrinerung', in Imbert Schenk et at (eds), *Film – Kino – Zuschauer* Marburg: Schüren, 2010. (Translation by Veronika Rall)

'*Snow White* in 1930s Britain'. *Journal of British Cinema and Television*, vol.7, no.2 (2010).

2011

'*Snow White* in Grossbritannien (1938)', in Gudrun Sommer et al (eds), *Orte filmischen Wissens: Filmkulttur und Filmvermittlung im Zeitalter digitaler Netzwerke*. Marburg: Schüren, 2011. (Translation by Christine N. Brinckmann)

'What to do with cinema memory?' in Richard Maltby, Daniel Biltereyst and Philippe Meers (eds), *Explorations in New Cinema History: Approaches and Case Studies*. Malden, MA: Blackwell, 2011.

2013

'Home is where we start from', in Annette Kuhn (ed.), *Little Madnesses: Winnicott, Transitional Phenomena and Cultural Experience*. London: Bloomsbury, 2013.

Appendix 1 Academic Publications

2014

'Sloiki po dzemie i cliffhangery: brytyscy seniorzy wspominaja dzieciece wizyty w kinie', in Konrad Klejsa and Magdalena Sryusz-Wolska (eds), *Badanie widowni filmowej*. Warsaw: Wydawictwo Naukowe, 2014. (Translation by Bartosz Kazana)

2017

(with Daniel Biltereyst and Philippe Meers) *Memory Studies* vol.10, no.1, 2017. Special issue on Cinemagoing, Film Experience and Memory.

(with Daniel Biltereyst and Philippe Meers), 'Memories of cinemagoing and film experience: an introduction', *Memory Studies*, vol.10, no.1, (2017).

2019

Daniel Biltereyst, 'Film history, cultural memory and the experience of cinema: an interview with Annette Kuhn', in Richard Maltby, Daniel Biltereyst and Philippe Meers (eds), *The Routledge Companion to New Cinema History*. London: Routledge, 2019.

Academic publications drawing on CCINTB archival assets

Sarah Street, *British Cinema in Documents*. London: Routledge, 2000.

Sarah J. Smith, *Children, Cinema and Censorship: from Dracula to the Dead End Kids*. London: I. B. Tauris, 2005.

Gil Toffell, *Jews, Cinema and Public Life in Interwar Britain*. London: Palgrave, 2018.

Appendix 2
The Cinema Memory Archive

IN THE COURSE of Cinema Culture in 1930s Britain (CCINTB) a wealth of 1990s participant-generated material was gathered and recorded, forming a collection comprising close to two hundred hours of in-depth interviews conducted with 1930s cinemagoers living in four areas of mainland Britain; over three hundred postal questionnaires completed by 1930s cinemagoers from across the UK; hundreds of letters, essays and written memoirs received from interviewees and questionnaire respondents; and more than two hundred items of cinemagoing memorabilia and artefacts from the 1930s (diaries, postcard collections, scrapbooks, cinema programmes, posters, film annuals, magazines). In 2006 the collection was deposited in Special Collections at Lancaster University Library, along with a corpus of non-participant materials: primary and secondary historical source materials on 1930s cinemagoing; research notes; project administration records; progress reports; drafts of conference papers and publications and suchlike.

Although the collection was subsequently consulted by a few researchers, it remained uncatalogued and incompletely organised until the UK Arts and Humanities Research Council funded a successor project to CCINTB, Cinema Memory and the Digital Archive: 1930s Britain and Beyond (CMDA), for a three-year period starting in

Exploring Cinema Memory

CINEMA MEMORY AND THE DIGITAL ARCHIVE
1930S BRITAIN & BEYOND

ABOUT · CCINTB PROJECT · THE ARCHIVE · SEARCH THE ARCHIVE · OUTPUTS & OUTREACH · NEWS & BLOG

OVERVIEW

Welcome to the site! *Cinema Memory and the Digital Archive* (CMDA) builds on 'Cinema Culture in 1930s Britain' (CCINTB), a pioneering nationwide inquiry into cinemagoing and everyday life in the interwar years that was conducted during the 1990s and early 2000s. The project has made data from the original investigation widely accessible and is extending its findings through comparative and interdisciplinary inquiries into the nature of cinema memory as a distinct variant of cultural memory, drawing on and developing a range of digital tools.

Further details on the background of CMDA and its aims can be found on the 'About' page.

We hope you enjoy exploring the collection. Visit the Using this site page if you would like to familiarise yourself with site structure and functionality.

Examples from our 'Picturegoer Postcards' collection

The CMDA website landing page: www.lancaster.ac.uk/fass/projects/cmda/

2019. Taking advantage of developments over the intervening years in digital technologies, digital humanities and archive development, CMDA's objectives include archiving and digitising materials in the CCINTB collection.

The overarching aim is to make the materials accessible in both physical and digital formats in a newly created Cinema Memory Archive: this has involved organising, cataloguing, conserving, storing and digitising materials in the collection.[1]

At the same time, the CMDA website has been created as the most immediately visible face of the CMDA project, designed to showcase, and to facilitate interrogation of, participant-generated materials in the digital archive: https://www.lancaster.ac.uk/fass/projects/cmda/

CCINTB core interviews can be accessed via the website in both audio and transcript formats along with hundreds of participant documents (including letters, essays and questionnaires) viewable as both digital scans and transcripts. In addition, numerous items of cinema memorabilia (such as postcard collections, photo albums and scrapbooks) can be browsed.

The website comprises six areas

- **About**: this area contains an overview of the CMDA project, information about the project team and funders, information on using the site, a copyright notice and a guide to citation of materials.[2]

- **CCINTB Project**: this provides details of the original Cinema Culture in 1930s Britain project, including information on its underlying research design and a detailed timeline showing what steps ultimately led to the CMDA project.

- **The Archive**: this area provides background information on the key data sources of CCINTB, namely questionnaires, interviews and documents, as well as a subsection ('CCINTB Places') devoted to CCINTB fieldwork locations; and a further subsection that provides links to various scanned items of 1930s film-related memorabilia. These latter are presented either in 'flipbook' or 'slideshow' format, with PDF versions also made available where applicable.

- **Search the Archive**: three search engine mechanisms have been created to enable visitors to search the archive: Keyword Search, Participant Attribute Search and Memorabilia search.

- **Outputs & Outreach**: this page lists all publications, creative outputs and events undertaken by the project team, as well as details of creative works commissioned by the project.

- **News & Blog**: this houses the project blog, which has been used both to publicise events and to publish blog posts on project-related research themes; and the embedded project Twitter feed.

A PDF user guide for the website, including instructions on searching the archive, can be viewed and downloaded at https://www.lancaster.ac.uk/fass/projects/cmda/wp-content/uploads/2022/07/CMDASite_UserGuide.pdf

Consulting materials in the physical archive can be arranged by contacting Special Collections at Lancaster University Library.

Notes

[1] The schema devised for accessioning and cataloguing materials for the Cinema Memory Archive is explained in Julia McDowell and Annie Nissen, 'A Digital Archive Is Born: Revisiting the "Cinema Culture in 1930s Britain" Collection', *Alphaville* 21 (2021): 144-159.

[2] https://www.lancaster.ac.uk/fass/projects/cmda/index.php/about/citation-referencing-guide/ [accessed 31 December 2022]

Bibliography

Allen, Robert C. (1998). 'From exhibition to reception: reflections on the audience in film history', in Annette Kuhn and Jackie Stacey (eds), *Screen Histories: a Screen Reader*. Oxford, Oxford University Press: 13-21.

Allen, Robert C. and Douglas Gomery (1985). *Film History: Theory and Practice*. New York, Alfred A. Knopf.

Ang, Ien (1985). *Watching Dallas: Soap Opera and the Melodramatic Imagination*. London, Routledge.

Barker, Martin (2019). 'How shall we measure our progress? On paradigms, metaphors and meetings in audience research', *Television & New Media* 20(2): 130–141.

Bergman, Anni (1995). 'From mother to the world outside: the use of space during the separation–individuation phase', in Simon A. Grolnick and Leonard S. Barkin (eds), *From Fantasy to Reality*. Northvale, NJ, Jason Aronson: 147-165.

Biltereyst, Daniel, Kathryn Lotze and Philippe Meers (2012). 'Triangulation in historical audience research: reflections and experiences from a multi-methodological research project on cinema audiences in Flanders', *Participations: Journal of Audience & Reception Studies* 9(2): 690–715.

Bilterseyt, Daniel, Richard Maltby and Philippe Meers (eds) (2019). *The Routledge Companion to New Cinema History*. London, Routledge.

Bobo, Jacqueline (1988). '*The Color Purple*: black women as cultural readers', in Deidre Pribram (ed.), *Female Spectators: Looking at Film and Television*. London, Verso: 90-109.

Bollas, Christopher (1993). 'The aesthetic moment and the search for transformation', in Peter L. Rudnytsky (ed.), *Transitional Objects and Potential Spaces: The Literary Uses of D.W. Winnicott*. New York, Columbia University Press: 40-49.

Burgin, Victor (2004). *The Remembered Film*. London, Reaktion Books.

Casetti, Francesco (2009). 'Filmic experience', *Screen* 50(1): 56-66.

Casey, Edward (1987). *Remembering: A Phenomenological Study*. Bloomington, IN, Indiana University Press.

Davis, Madeleine and David Wallbridge (1990). *Boundary and Space: An Introduction to the Work of D.W. Winnicott*. London, Karnac.

De Certeau, Michel (1984). *The Practice of Everyday Life* (trans. S Rendall). Berkeley, CA, University of California Press.

Egan, Kate, Martin Ian Smith and Jamie Terrill (eds) (2022). *Researching Historical Screen Audiences*. Edinburgh, Edinburgh University Press.

Engberg, Maria and Jay David Bolter (2017). 'Mobile cinematics', in Pepita Hesselberth and Maria Poulaki (eds), *Compact Cinematics: The Moving Image in the Age of Bit-Sized Media*. New York, Bloomsbury: 165-173.

Forman, Henry James (1933). *Our Movie-Made Children.* New York, MacMillan.

Freud, Sigmund (1984). 'Beyond the pleasure principle (1920)', *Pelican Freud Library,* vol. 11. Harmondsworth, Penguin: 269-338.

Freud, Sigmund (2001). ' "A child is being beaten": a contribution to the origin of sexual perversions (1919)', in *The Standard Edition of the Complete Psychological Works of Sigmund Freud XVII.* trans. and ed. James Strachey. London, Vintage: 177-204.

Grolnick, Simon A. and Leonard S. Barkin (eds) (1995). *From Fantasy to Reality.* Northvale, NJ, Jason Aronson.

Hodgkin, Katharine and Susannah Radstone (eds) (2003). *Contested Pasts: The Politics of Memory.* London, Routledge.

Jancovich, Mark, Lucy Faire and Sarah Stubbings (2003). *The Place of the Audience: Cultural Geographies of Film Consumption.* London, British Film Institute.

Kuhn, Annette (1984). 'Women's genres', *Screen* 25(1): 18–28.

Kuhn, Annette (1994) *Women's Pictures: Feminism and Cinema.* 2nd ed. London, Verso.

Kuhn, Annette (1996). 'Cinema culture and femininity in the 1930s', in Christine Gledhill and Gillian Swanson (eds) *Nationalising Femininity.* Manchester, Manchester University Press: 177–192.

Kuhn, Annette (1999). 'Memories of cinema-going in the 1930s', *Journal of Popular British Cinema* 2: 100-120.

Kuhn, Annette (2000). 'A journey through memory', in Susannah Radstone (ed.), *Memory and Methodology.* Oxford, Berg: 179-196.

Kuhn, Annette (2002). *An Everyday Magic: Cinema and Cultural Memory.* London, Bloomsbury.

Kuhn, Annette (2002). *Family Secrets: Acts of Memory and Imagination.* London, Verso.

Kuhn, Annette (2004). 'Heterotopia, heterochronia: place and time in cinema memory', *Screen* 45 (2): 106-114.

Kuhn, Annette (2005). 'Thresholds: film as film and the aesthetic experience', *Screen* 46(4): 401-414.

Kuhn, Annette (2010). *'Snow White* in the 1930s', *Journal of British Cinema and Television* 7(2): 183-199.

Kuhn, Annette (2010). 'Cinematic experience, film space and the child's world', *Canadian Journal of Film Studies* 19(2): 82-98.

Kuhn, Annette (2010). 'Memory texts and memory work: performances of memory in and with visual media', *Memory Studies*: 298-313.

Kuhn, Annette (2011). 'What to do with cinema memory?' in Richard Maltby, Daniel Biltereyst and Philippe Meers (eds), *Explorations in New Cinema History: Approaches and Case Studies.* Malden, MA: Wiley-Blackwell: 85-97.

Kuhn, Annette (2013). *Little Madnesses: Winnicott: Transitional Phenomena and Cultural Experience.* London, Bloomsbury.

Kuhn, Annette (2020). 'Quest narratives: the cinematic experience, film space and transitional phenomena', *Free Associations* 79: 77-89.

Kuhn, Annette, Daniel Biltereyst and Philippe Meers (2017). 'Memories of cinema-going and film experience: an introduction', *Memory Studies* 10 (1): 3-16.

McDowell, Julia and Annie Nissen (2021). 'A digital archive is born: revisiting the "Cinema Culture in 1930s Britain" Collection', *Alphaville* 21: 144-159.

Mahler, Margaret S. (1979). *The Selected Papers of Margaret S. Mahler, Vol II: Separation-Individuation*. New York, Jason Aronson.

Maltby, Richard (2011). 'New cinema histories', in Richard Maltby, Daniel Biltereyst and Philippe Meers (eds), *Explorations in New Cinema History: Approaches and Case Studies*. Malden, MA, Wiley-Blackwell: 3–40.

Maltby, Richard and Melvyn Stokes (eds) (2007). *Hollywood Abroad: Audiences and Cultural Exchange*. London, British Film Institute.

Maltby, Richard, Daniel Biltereyst and Philippe Meers (eds) (2011). *Explorations in New Cinema History: Approaches and Case Studies*. Malden, MA, Wiley-Blackwell.

Maltby, Richard, Melvyn Stokes and Robert C. Allen (eds) (2007). *Going to the Movies: Hollywood and the Social Experience of Cinema*. Exeter, University of Exeter Press.

Marks, Laura U. (1999). *The Skin of the Film: Intercultural Cinema, Embodiment and the Senses*. Durham, NC, Duke University Press.

Meers, Philippe, Daniel Biltereyst and Lies Van De Vijver (2010). 'Memories, movies and cinema-going: an oral history project on film culture in Flanders (Belgium)', in Irmbert Schenk,

Margrit Tröhler and Yvonne Zimmerman (eds), *Film – Kino – Zuschauer: Filmrezeption/ Film – Cinema – Spectator: Film Reception*. Marburg, Schüren: 319–337.

Meers, Philippe, Daniel Biltereyst and Lies Van De Vijver (2010). 'Metropolitan vs. rural cinema-going in Flanders, 1925–75', *Screen* 51/3: 272–280.

Metz, Christian (1982). *The Imaginary Signifier: Psychoanalysis and the Cinema*. Trans. Celia Britton, Annwyl Williams, Ben Brewster and Alfred Guzzetti. Bloomington, IN, Indiana University Press.

Milner, Marion (1993). 'The role of illusion in symbol formation', in Peter L. Rudnytsky (ed.), *Transitional Objects and Potential Spaces: The Literary Uses of D.W. Winnicott*. New York, Columbia University Press: 13-39.

Milner, Marion (1987). 'The framed gap', in *The Suppressed Madness of Sane Men*. Hove, Brunner-Routledge: 79-82.

Philo, Chris and Hester Parr (2003). 'Introducing psychoanalytic geographies', *Social and Cultural Geography* 4 (3): 283-293.

Nowell-Smith, Geoffrey (1990). 'On history and the cinema', *Screen* 31(2): 160-171

Portelli, Alessandro (1981). 'The peculiarities of oral history', *History Workshop* 12: 99.

Puwar, Nirmal (2007). 'Social cinema scenes', *Space and Culture* 10(2): 253-270.

Radstone, Susannah and Katharine Hodgkin (eds) (2003), *Regimes of Memory*. London, Routledge.

Radway, Janice (1984). *Reading the Romance: Women, Patriarchy and Popular Literature.* Chapel Hill, NC, University of North Carolina Press.

Rose, Gilbert J. (1995). 'The creativity of everyday life', in Simon A. Grolnick and Leonard S. Barkin (eds), *Between Reality and Fantasy: Winnicott's Concepts of Transitional Objects and Phenomena.* Northvale, NJ, Jason Aronson: 347-362.

Rudnytsky, Peter L. (ed.) (1993). *Transitional Objects and Potential Spaces: The Literary Uses of D.W. Winnicott.* New York, Columbia University Press.

Sabbadini, Andrea (2011). 'Cameras, mirrors and the bridge space: a Winnicottian lens on cinema', *Projections* 5(1): 17-30.

Silverstone, Roger (1994). *Television and Everyday Life.* London, Routledge.

Stacey, Jackie (1993). 'Textual obsessions: method, memory and researching female spectatorship', *Screen* 34(3): 260-274.

Stacey, Jackie (1994). *Star Gazing: Hollywood Cinema and Female Spectatorship.* London, Routledge.

Stokes, Melvyn and Richard Maltby (eds) (1999). *American Movie Audiences: From the Turn of the Century to the Early Sound Era.* London, British Film Institute.

Stokes, Melvyn and Richard Maltby (eds) (1999). *Identifying Hollywood's Audiences: Cultural Identity and the Movies.* London, British Film Institute.

Stokes, Melvyn and Richard Maltby (eds) (2001). *Hollywood Spectatorship: Changing Perceptions of Cinema Audiences.* London, British Film Institute.

Stokes, Melvyn, Matthew Jones and Emma Pett (2022). *Cinema Memories: A People's History of Cinema-Going in 1960s Britain.* London, Bloomsbury.

Taranger, Marie-Claude (1991). 'Une mémoire de seconde main? Film, emprunt et référence dans le récit de vie', *Hors-Cadre* 9.

Taylor, Helen (1989). *Scarlett's Women: Gone With the Wind and its Female Fans.* London, Virago Press.

Treveri Gennari, Daniela, Catherine O'Rawe, Danielle Hipkins, Silvia Dibeltulo and Sarah Culhane (2021). *Italian Cinema Audiences: Histories and Memories of Cinema-going in Post-war Italy.* New York, Bloomsbury Academic.

Willis, Paul (2016). *Learning to Labour.* London, Routledge.

Winnicott, D. W. (1986). *Home Is Where We Start From.* Harmondsworth, Penguin.

Winnicott, D.W. (1989). 'The fate of the transitional object (1959)', in Clare Winnicott, Ray Shepherd and Madeleine Davis (eds), *Psycho-Analytic Explorations.* London, Karnac Books: 53-58.

Winnicott, D. W. (1991). 'Transitional objects and transitional phenomena', *Playing and Reality.* London, Routledge: 1-34.

Winnicott, D.W. (1991). 'The use of an object and relating through identifications', *Playing and Reality.* London, Routledge: 115-127.

Winnicott, D. W. (1991). 'The location of cultural experience', *Playing and Reality.* London, Routledge: 128-139.

Winnicott, D. W. (2002). *Through Paediatrics to Psychoanalysis: Collected Papers.* London, Karnac Books.

Young, Robert M. (1989). 'Transitional phenomena: production and consumption', in Barry Richards (ed.), *Crises of the Self: Further Essays on Psychoanalysis and Politics.* London, Free Association Books: 57-72.

Zittoun, Tania (2013). 'On the use of a film: cultural experiences as symbolic resources', in Annette Kuhn (ed.), *Little Madnesses: Winnicott, Transitional Phenomena and Cultural Experience.* London, Bloomsbury: 135–147.

Index

A
aesthetic moment 97, 98, 103
All Quiet on the Western Front (1930) 45
Allen, Robert C. 17
An Everyday Magic 9, 11, 17, 20, 41, 83, 112

B
Battle of the Somme (1916) 45
Bielby, Denise 106
Biltereyst, Daniel 9-10, 17
Bobo, Jacqueline 16
Burgin, Victor 41, 42, 44, 46, 47, 51, 53, 85, 86, 87

C
Certeau, Michel de 64
Cinema Culture in 1930s Britain 11, 13, 15, 17, 27, 63, 79, 117
    research design 18, 20, 42, 80
cinema/film distinction 61ff, 74
cinema memory
    and aging 28, 106
    and childhood 36, 37, 65, 92
    and collective experience 91
    and cultural memory 38, 41, 42, 52, 56, 65, 93
    and embodiment 36, 37, 38, 46, 54, 71, 86
    and emotion 46
    and primary process 47, 87, 88
    and secondary revision 90
    and transcendence 106
    anecdotal 50, 53, 89
    as discourse 42, 43, 89
    fear in 36, 44
    formulaic tropes in 92
    future of 22, 74
    implanted 50, 89-90
    modes of 21, 43-46, 85ff, 104-105
    place in 19, 20, 64, 65, 71, 72, 82, 83, 92, 100
    repetitive 53, 91
    themes in 20, 42, 43
    time in 27, 31-36
    'walking tour' in 65, 67, 68, 69, 82-83
cinema in the world/the world in cinema 29, 30, 31-36, 38, 72, 100-102, 103, 105
Cinema Memory and the Digital Archive 10, 22, 117-118
cinematic apparatus 76
cliffhangers 20, 35, 38
Color Purple, The (1985) 16
continuous programming 32, 33, 34, 49
cultural experience 21, 22, 63, 97, 98, 99, 100, 104, 106, 107
    and ageing 106-107
    cinema as 41, 87
cultural studies 80

D
Davies, Terence 42

E
ethnohistory 17, 18, 79

F

feeling-memory 101, 103, 105
female audience 16, 18
filmic space 101
Four Sons (1928) 34, 45, 89
Freud, Sigmund
  fort/da game 68
  on fantasy 46, 87

G

Gomery, Douglas 17
Gone With the Wind (1939) 16, 23, 79

H

Harrington, C. Lee 106
heterotopia (Foucault) 31
'horrific' films 45

J

jam jars 37, 54, 90, 92
Jancovich, Mark 17

K

Karloff, Boris 44, 45, 49
Kid, The (1921) 50
King Kong (1933) 51, 90

L

Last Metro, The/Le Dernier Métro (1980) 52

M

Meers, Philippe 17
memory text 20, 47, 48, 87
memory work 15, 18, 19, 42, 57, 65, 83, 97
Metz, Christian 47
Milner, Marion 99
Mummy, The (1933) 44, 45, 49

N

New Cinema History 14, 104
Nowell-Smith, Geoffrey 27

O

Object-Relations psychoanalysis 21, 63, 68, 69, 97, 98, 99, 100, 104, 105, 107
  and cultural experience 99, 100, 104, 106
oral history 55, 80, 92

P

place-memory see cinema memory, place in; topographical memory
Portelli, Sandro 55
potential space 98, 99, 105, 106
Puwar, Nirmal 55, 92

R

Remembered Film, The 41, 53, 85
remembered images/scenes 43, 44, 46, 56, 86, 88, 105
revisionist film history 17, 19
Rose, Gilbert 99

INDEX

S

'Screen Dreams' 41, 51, 53
separation–individuation 68, 71, 73, 75
'sequence-image' 44, 47, 48, 85, 87
Seventh Heaven (1927) 49
silent cinema 45
Silverstone, Roger 75
Singin' in the Rain (1952) 50
situated memories 43, 49, 52, 56, 88, 90, 105
Snow White and the Seven Dwarfs (1937) 50, 89
social cinema scenes 21, 55, 90, 92, 93
Stacey, Jackie 16, 79

T

Taranger, Marie-Claude 51
Taylor, Helen 16, 79

topographical memory 20, 21, 65, 71
topographical memory talk 20, 67, 83
transitional object 63, 64, 68, 69, 70, 71, 75, 98, 99
 and new media 75
 television as 75
transitional space 70, 71, 76
triangulation 18, 41

W

Winnicott, D.W. 63, 68, 69, 70, 71, 76, 98, 99, 106

Z

Zittoun, Tania 100, 106

133